PALM BEACH ENTERTAINING

Creating Occasions to Remember

PALM BEACH ENTERTAINING

Creating Occasions to Remember

ANNIE FALK

WITH VICTORIA AMORY, AIME DUNSTAN,
AND DAPHNE NIKOLOPOULOS

FOREWORD BY ALAIN DUCASSE
PHOTOGRAPHS BY JERRY RABINOWITZ

RIZZOLI
NEW YORK

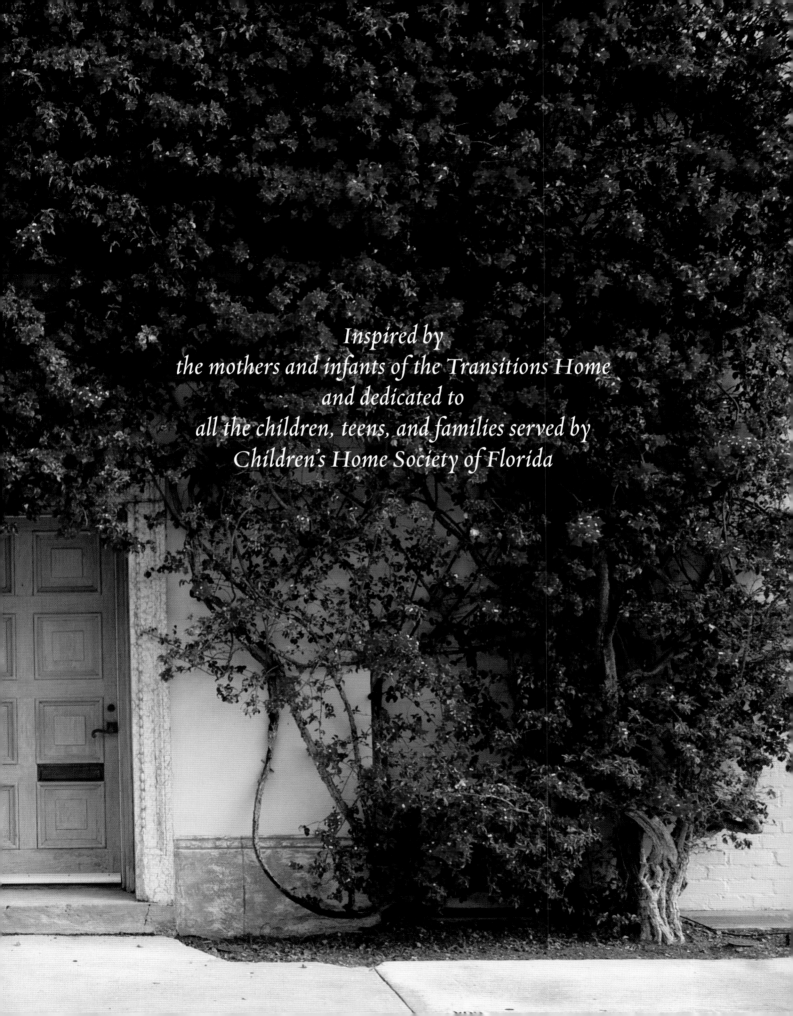

*Inspired by
the mothers and infants of the Transitions Home
and dedicated to
all the children, teens, and families served by
Children's Home Society of Florida*

MESSAGE FROM DAVID A. BUNDY

SINCE ITS EARLIEST DAYS, Children's Home Society of Florida (CHS) has been blessed to have the generous support of men and women who care deeply about improving the lives of abused, abandoned, and neglected children. This book is yet another example of what a determined, committed group of people can accomplish when they come together to change the lives of children who want nothing more than love, security, and protection.

CHS is indebted to the many caring people who made this project come to life. Though it is impossible to name every person who contributed to this effort, I would like to extend particular thanks to Annie Falk, who conceived the initiative, and her colleagues Victoria Amory, Aime Dunstan, and Daphne Nikolopoulos. These women have poured their hearts, souls, and amazing talent into producing a book that will have lasting impact on the lives of children in CHS care.

To everyone who made this book possible, and to everyone who has made it part of their collection, CHS thanks you.

With warmest regards,

David A. Bundy

David A. Bundy
President/CEO
Children's Home Society of Florida

ABOUT CHILDREN'S HOME SOCIETY OF FLORIDA

MISSION: EMBRACING CHILDREN. INSPIRING LIVES.

Children's Home Society of Florida (CHS) is a beacon of hope for abused, abandoned, and neglected children and for families wanting to grow and thrive. Founded in Jacksonville in 1902 to find loving homes for orphans, CHS has since grown and evolved to serve children, teens, and families throughout Florida.

Building upon our sterling reputation for adoption services, CHS has become a state and national leader in family-centered and home-based services, focusing on protecting children, empowering teens and young adults to live independent, successful lives, and building strong, healthy families. With an increased focus on preventing child abuse and neglect, CHS aims to ensure every child is safe, healthy, and prepared for life.

Led by the desire to break the tragic generational cycle of abuse and neglect for more and more children, CHS offers a myriad of services in nearly every community in the state. In addition to our stellar adoption services, we offer foster care, emergency shelter and group home care, family and individual counseling, mentoring, and so much more. As the premier child welfare organization in Florida, CHS has maintained national accreditation by the Council on Accreditation since 1982 and has been honored as a Congressional Angel in Adoption by the Congressional Coalition on Adoption Institute.

In Palm Beach County, CHS's South Coastal Division has been helping children and families since 1964. Focused on every child's safety and well-being, we emphasize prevention efforts, that is, protecting children from ever suffering the tragedies of abuse or neglect, by working with entire families and connecting parents with the tools and community resources they need to succeed and to appropriately care for their children.

We also work with families in crisis, offering intervention services that work quickly to deal with the core issues that triggered the crisis, upholding our priority to keep children safe at all times. And, with a renewed focus on independent and transitional living, CHS is committed to helping more young adults—many of whom have spent the majority of their lives in foster care—learn the skills and gain the confidence necessary to lead independent, self-sufficient lives. Every year, our South Coastal Division helps more than 25,000 children, youth, and families in Palm Beach County. Though our services may evolve to meet the changing needs of our community, our commitment to protecting children and strengthening families will never falter.

INTRODUCTION

SINCE THE GILDED AGE AND THE ERA of Henry Morrison Flagler, Palm Beach has had an aura of mystique, wealth, and glamour that has survived through the decades. It also has been heightened to mythic proportions by the likes of the Kennedys, the Duke and Duchess of Windsor, and even photographer Slim Aarons. Perhaps less celebrated is the heart and soul of Palm Beach: its residents and their desire to give their talent, time, and wealth for the good of others.

Bringing the famous Palm Beach lifestyle to life, *Palm Beach Entertaining* is an invitation to meet some of the most illustrious leaders from the worlds of fashion, finance, design, and the arts; the most celebrated members of society, both in Palm Beach and on an international stage. These influential party-givers are supremely creative and generous; collectively, they are the crème de la crème of Palm Beach society and the essence of all that makes Palm Beach such an exceptional place to live, work, and entertain.

Join me for an unprecedented entrée into the private homes and parties of these hosts, where they share their recipes, resources, colorful anecdotes from parties past, and advice and tips for stylish entertaining, whether formal or informal, traditional or avant-garde. At each party there is a uniqueness that is magical and transports one away from everyday life for a few hours: memories of a spring past are evoked by a table setting filled with tulips of every imaginable color; guests take a trip to the South with comforting and homey tomato "pudding" and cheesy homemade grits; a moist and decadent chocolate bundt cake recalls favorite childhood treats; an exotic getaway among friends is enjoyed with a Moroccan-inspired menu. What makes these gatherings so memorable is the key to success for any event—thoughtfulness and attention to detail.

Entertaining plays an important role in life, allowing us to enjoy the pleasure of the company of family and friends. Together, we create those luminous moments, the ones that ultimately will matter the most, creating memories we will reflect upon with great happiness for years to come. Whether you are a seasoned party veteran or new to entertaining, I know you will be inspired, as I have, by the portraits of beautifully appointed tables, elaborately decorated homes, lush floral arrangements, heirloom china, and unique menus. I am sure you will enjoy discovering new and exciting ideas for your own gatherings, collecting the go-to recipes used by well-seasoned hosts, and accessing their most prized resources. A host's primary goal is for their guests to enjoy a memorable, enriching evening and these pages help define the nuances of doing just that.

Many years ago, when I imagined entertaining in my own home, I didn't necessarily think I would be cooking the meal: I didn't know how to cook. But that all changed over a meal at Lutèce, Manhattan's renowned French restaurant. My fiancé and I had a candid conversation about what constitutes a dream spouse. Thankfully, his only regret was to have fallen in love with a woman who couldn't cook. Before our tea was served, I slipped into the kitchen and told Lutèce's chef and owner, Andre Soltner, that I needed to learn to cook, and quickly. He patiently asked if it mattered where I studied, and he promised to meet me at my table after dinner with some ideas—and petit fours, of course. Before I knew it, I was packing my bags for the South of France to spend a week with legendary chef Roger Verge at Le Moulin de Mougins, and about to embark upon a culinary adventure that would ignite a lifelong passion for cooking, dining, and entertaining.

Much of entertaining in Palm Beach is about charitable giving. When I was invited to chair Children's Home Society of Florida's "Ultimate Dinner Party," a fundraiser and variation on the progressive dinner party format, I was thrilled. CHS's mission is one close to my heart and the "Ultimate Dinner Party" is gracious entertaining at its finest. Chairing this event created a unique opportunity to combine my passion for entertaining with my commitment to humanitarian work, and it served as the inspiration for this book. In the spirit of Palm Beach, proceeds from this book will assist Children's Home Society of Florida.

Annie Falk

Annie Falk

FOREWORD

AS THE ARCHITECT FRANK LLOYD WRIGHT once said, "Dining is, and always was, a great artistic opportunity." Indeed. Dining, in its most authentic expression, is a joy that transcends the quotidian, encroaching, like art, on the realm of the sublime. And yet that authenticity has at its heart simplicity—an effortless alchemy of honest food and imagination, presented with a personal touch and enjoyed in good company.

Palm Beach Entertaining: Creating Occasions to Remember is an exquisite articulation of this very principle. The hosts and hostesses whose parties are showcased in this volume have an innate sense of celebrating the act of dining, not for its sake alone but for the whole experience. Dining, after all, involves all the senses. Who among us has not been seduced by the perfume of a suckling pig roasting in the oven, or by the delicate ring of wine glasses brought together in a toast, or by the serene beauty of field flowers composed artfully at the center of the al fresco table?

The images, stories, anecdotes, tips, and recipes you will see in the pages of *Palm Beach Entertaining* weave a narrative of entertaining as individualistic expression. The food and the wine are central to the experience, of course, but the other details are just as important, for it is through these that the story is told. From the purposeful selection of tableware and the styling of centerpieces to the procurement of seasonal ingredients from their native source, the choices of these hosts reveal a local sensibility within a global understanding—the hallmark not only of the stylish, but also of the wise.

But there is another element at play here: the spirit of voluntarism. Palm Beach is a small but benevolent community, and philanthropy—the gift of time, talent, and treasure—

is very much a part of its DNA. This book is the manifestation of that spirit. Annie Falk, who conceived and produced *Palm Beach Entertaining* for the benefit of Children's Home Society of Florida, has had a longstanding commitment to giving on a local and national level, cohosting important events alongside the world's most recognized names in entertainment, fashion, and society. So devoted is she to philanthropy that she has made it a family tradition, instilling the notion of voluntarism in her own children from an early age, and together they have participated in humanitarian projects all over the globe.

Annie's vision for this book went well beyond guiding readers inside the private soirees of the best-known Palm Beachers. She wanted to show a more intimate side of Palm Beach, where food and wine become the catalyst for effervescent conversation, the sharing of ideas and ideals, and memories in the making.

To execute her vision, Annie assembled a truly talented cast of contributors. The chefs who have helped shape menus and perfect recipes, the editors who have brought these parties to life for the reader, and the photographer who has so beautifully captured intimate moments, all have volunteered their time in the spirit of giving back. A noble endeavor, indeed.

The pages that follow show a different side of Palm Beach than the one imagined by much of the world. There is opulence, yes; but there is also soul. The essence of savoir-faire imbues Palm Beach, adding texture and color to its fiber. That is evident in this volume, sometimes in overt gestures, sometimes in barely discernible winks. You will enjoy reading it, as I have.

Alain Ducasse

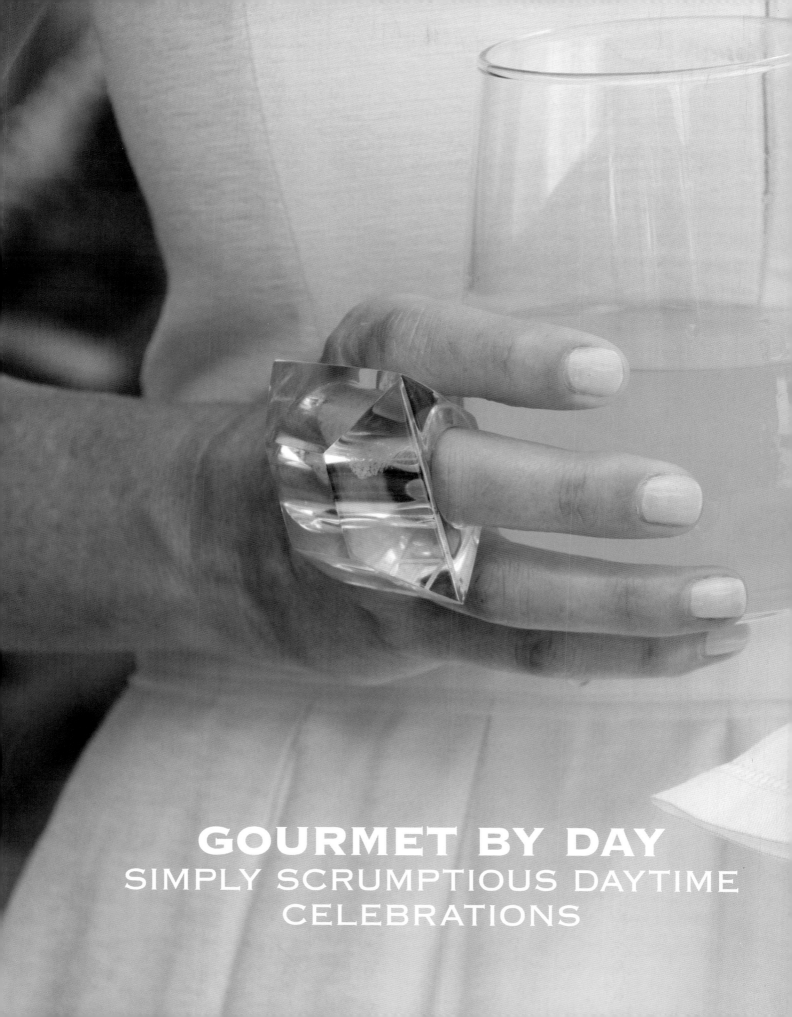

GOURMET BY DAY
SIMPLY SCRUMPTIOUS DAYTIME CELEBRATIONS

GATHERING AT THE LAKE HOUSE
TALBOTT MAXEY AND KIT PANNILL

AT THE HEIGHT OF THE SEASON, Palm Beach is the land of parties, parties, and more parties, but there are still moments when the most jaded partygoer gets excited about an invitation—and that is precisely what happens when Talbott Maxey calls, inviting you to join her and her beautiful mother, Kit Pannill, for a gathering at the Lake House. Set on Palm Beach's Intracoastal Waterway and surrounded by beautiful gardens, hundreds of tropical blooms, and a genuine feeling of Southern hospitality, the setting is irresistible. Perhaps the only thing more irresistible is Kit's home-cooked buffet, which some of Palm Beach's toniest residents have been known to crave.

Most parties at the Lake House are thrown for honored guests in celebration of life's happiest milestones, such as bridal showers, anniversaries, baby showers, and, of course, birthdays. Talbott says, "The guest list depends on the event. If we are hosting a baby shower, then we invite friends of the mother-to-be. Last season we hosted a dinner for a guest speaker of the Society of the Four Arts and invited people in the community who we thought would be interested in meeting the speaker."

On that evening, Kit had another engagement, but she cooked before heading off to her party. "I stayed and hosted our guest, who was so amazed and thankful for a home-cooked meal," she says.

"Normally, this type of gathering would happen in a club or restaurant, but this was so much more intimate," says Talbott.

"Whatever the occasion," Kit says, "we hope to have an interesting group of people who will enjoy talking to each other, and not always the same people. Talbott enjoys putting the guest list together, and we talk about it."

Kit Pannill (center), Talbott Maxey (right), and friends

Put together an interesting group of people who will enjoy talking to each other, and mix young and old.

Don't always invite the same crowd. If you are having your bridge friends over, invite a few ladies you play tennis with. Your friends will enjoy meeting new friends.

Serve a home-cooked meal; it is so rare these days, and guests really enjoy it.

If you are hosting a party in honor of a dear friend, add something fanciful to the table using her image. Photoshop her portrait and use it on the place cards or menu. When guests sit at the table, there is conversation and laughter immediately.

Decorate the table with something from the garden. We love to use our potted succulents to add color and complement the china.

Always stocked in Kit's freezer: homemade chocolate pie and homemade pecan pie.

No e-mails or text messages; Talbott prefers to call and personally invite guests. This way she knows exactly who is joining. Those who accept will receive a beautiful card with the date and time—just a reminder. She also has been known to enlist the help of her stepfather, William Pannill, who loves to design and create original graphics for invitations, place cards, T-shirts, or other memorable party favors.

"Bill loves to make up fun things using the guest of honor's image," Kit says. "Everyone loves it. He has created books and movies from party photos." It is a personal touch that no one forgets.

Setting the table is something mother and daughter do together. Talbott loves hosting parties with her mom. It is their special way of spending time together. For today's luncheon, the ladies exit the orchid house carrying three strawberry pots filled with succulents grown by Kit. The subtle colors help determine the china and linens for the event.

Talbott begins to return calls from guests needing directions or advice on appropriate attire as Kit enters the kitchen to check on her pecan pie. Actually, there are two: pecan and chocolate. "I usually make two of each pie and freeze one of each; this way, I have something great to bring a sick friend or a hostess," she says.

In a decade when everyone is time-starved, it is so nourishing to settle back and enjoy a home-cooked meal, surrounded by flowers your hostess has grown and arranged. It feels like home.

ROASTED CAPRESE SALAD

Sometimes simple is simply the best. This salad is easy to make, rich in flavor, and presents beautifully. It's perfect for a buffet and looks gorgeous on the table, too.

Serves 8

16	large plum tomatoes, halved lengthwise, seeds (not cores) removed
¼	cup extra-virgin olive oil, plus more for drizzling
1½	tablespoons aged balsamic vinegar
2	large cloves garlic, minced
2	teaspoons sugar
	Salt and freshly ground black pepper
1½	pounds fresh salted mozzarella
16	leaves fresh basil

Preheat the oven to 275°F.

On a cookie sheet, arrange the tomatoes cut side up in a single layer. Drizzle with the olive oil and vinegar. Sprinkle the garlic and sugar over the top and season with salt and pepper.

Place in the oven and roast for about 2 hours, or until the tomatoes begin to caramelize. Remove from the oven and cool to room temperature.

Slice the mozzarella the same size as the tomatoes. To serve, layer the tomatoes alternately with the mozzarella on a decorative platter and scatter the basil on top. Season with salt and pepper and a drizzle of olive oil. Serve at room temperature.

SHRIMP SALAD

This salad, while lovely on the buffet, is a perfect warm-weather lunch or dinner. You can prepare it in advance and refrigerate it overnight; add the dill just before serving.

Serves 8

3	pounds peeled deveined shrimp, cooked, cooled, and cut in half
1¼	cups mayonnaise
2	tablespoons orange zest
2	tablespoons orange juice
1½	tablespoons white wine vinegar
	Salt and freshly ground black pepper
2	tablespoons capers, rinsed and dried
2	tablespoons minced red onion
2	tablespoons minced fresh dill

Place the shrimp in a large decorative salad bowl.

In a small bowl, whisk together the mayonnaise, orange zest, orange juice, and vinegar. Season with salt and pepper. Add the shrimp to the sauce and toss. Stir in the capers and red onions and season with salt and pepper.

Cover with plastic wrap and allow to rest for 30 minutes at room temperature or for up to 6 hours refrigerated. Add the dill just before serving and mix well.

Opposite: Kit's Tomato "Pudding"
Bottom left: Roasted Caprese Salad
Bottom Right: Cheese Grits with Kit's
Tomato "Pudding," Shrimp Salad, Ham Rolls

CHEESE GRITS

This delicious corn porridge can be served for breakfast, lunch, or dinner. For this party we smothered it with Kit's Tomato "Pudding" (recipe follows). Heaven.

Serves 8

2	cups chicken broth, preferably low-sodium
1	cup 5-minute grits (not instant)
1	cup milk
4	tablespoons (½ stick) unsalted butter
½	pound extra-sharp cheddar cheese
	Salt
	Pinch of ground cayenne

Bring the broth to a boil in a medium stock pot over medium-high heat. Gradually whisk in the grits, stirring constantly, and cook until thickened.

Slowly add the milk, stirring constantly. Add the butter and cheese and season with salt and the cayenne. Stir until creamy and the mixture is blended. Serve immediately.

KIT'S TOMATO "PUDDING"

This tomato "pudding" is sweet and delicious. It is lovely over grits and makes a wonderful side dish to roast pork. It is so flavorful you may just want to pour it over biscuits (see Club Colette's "Mrs. Pannill's Biscuits," page 206).

Serves 8

1	tablespoon extra-virgin olive oil
2	cups finely chopped onion
2	(28-ounce) cans whole peeled tomatoes, including liquid, sliced in half
5	to 6 slices white bread, crusts removed (preferably Pepperidge Farm Original), cubed
½	cup packed brown sugar
½	cup granulated sugar
½	cup (1 stick) unsalted butter, melted
	Freshly ground black pepper

Preheat the oven to 275°F.

Heat the oil in a medium skillet over medium heat. Add the onion and sauté until transparent, about 4 to 6 minutes; remove from the heat and set aside.

Place the tomatoes and bread in a deep casserole dish. Using your hands, squeeze the tomatoes and bread together until thoroughly combined. Stir in the sugars, butter, and sautéed onion and season with pepper.

Bake for 3 hours, or until you have a thick puddinglike consistency. Serve hot.

KIT'S PECAN PIE

A staple in Southern kitchens, this irresistibly sweet dessert is a perfect finish to a savory meal, and it freezes well. Serve as is or top with ice cream or bourbon-infused whipped cream.

Makes 1 (9-inch) pie; serves 8

1	to 1½ cups coarsely chopped pecans
1	(9-inch) prepared pie shell
6	tablespoons (¾ stick) unsalted butter, melted
1¼	cups packed light brown sugar
1	cup light or dark corn syrup
2	teaspoons vanilla extract
½	teaspoon orange zest
¼	teaspoon salt
3	large eggs, beaten
1	tablespoon bourbon

Preheat the oven to 350°F.

Spread the pecans over the pie shell.

Combine the melted butter, brown sugar, corn syrup, vanilla, orange zest, salt, eggs, and bourbon in a large bowl. Pour the pie filling over the pecans.

Place in the oven and bake for 45 to 50 minutes, or until the pie filling is firm around the edges and slightly soft but set in the center.

Cool completely on a wire rack, then transfer to a decorative platter to serve.

LUNCH WITH THE LADIES
VICTORIA AMORY

GROWING UP IN MADRID AND SEVILLE as the daughter of a Spanish count and countess, Victoria Amory learned the fine art of hospitality before she learned her multiplication tables. Dining, and making others feel welcome, at the family home was not reserved for special occasions; it was simply the done thing.

"We had a big family and many friends, and my parents entertained all the time," she says. "Once or twice a day, we all got together at our house in the country. That was the time we connected with each other."

She eventually left Spain to come to the United States but did not leave behind her passion for entertaining. "When I first moved here, I organized dinners in my apartment in New York, where I used the bed as the table," she says. "But that wasn't the point. I was being hospitable, and everyone came because it was fun."

Years later, Victoria's parties are still the coveted invitation in town. That's due in no small part to the intimacy of her home-cooked meals. She plans the menus, sources the fresh ingredients, and does all the cooking herself, whether it's simple hors d'oeuvres or a five-course feast. She doesn't see it as work; it's her gift to her friends. "It's my way of caring for my guests and being generous with my time," she says. "They can sense there is a part of me in the food they are eating."

For this ladies' lunch by the pool, she prepared a menu of simple salads. The recipes, all Victoria originals, are informed by her Mediterranean heritage and her travels.

The table, an informal but inspired composition in garden greens and ocean blues, honors the natural surroundings while providing for the comfort of her guests. "For lunch outside, I would not use superfine crystal or silver, which tends to shine too much in the sun," she notes. "I tend to use more rattan, wood, ceramics, and organic accents in colors that go with the outdoors."

Do as much as you can in advance, so when your guests come you are ready to entertain them.

Come up with a menu that is on par with your comfort level. Don't worry about being a perfectionist. It's all about the comforts of home and the welcome you are extending to your guests.

I use a lot of things I have around the house for table settings. I have used silver mugs from golf trophies, broccoli, ferns from the garden, and Chinese terra-cotta figures. Using objects you already have makes the table original and personal.

You don't need extravagant flowers on the table. I prefer to use things that will enhance the flavors of the food: flowers without much scent, greenery, fruit, vegetables, and so on.

Think multiuse. A soup tureen can double as a fruit bowl, stemless glasses as dessert coupes, and Moroccan tea glasses as pots de crème; shells can be filled with dip; banana leaves can be used to display canapés.

Have a good time doing it. If you, as the hostess, are miserable or hurried, your guests will be too.

There are plenty of nods to the outdoor setting: bamboo chairs wrapped with silk vines, a cachepot filled with potted annuals from the garden, and big straw hats to shade the ladies from the zealous Palm Beach sun. Her table scape is a study in effortless elegance, at once accessible and gracious. Mottahedeh's Blue Canton china, which she bought to go with the antique Chinese Blue Canton plates she inherited from her mother-in-law, pairs beautifully with glass demilune salad plates, while rattan-sleeved glasses and antique horn flatware add the organic dimension so essential to alfresco entertaining.

The key ingredient, though, is not tangible. "Being a great hostess is not about the food or the wine or the house," Victoria says. "It's about you—the time you spend making your friends comfortable at your home and sharing what you have."

BLUE CHEESE AND CARAMELIZED ONION TARTS

These tartlets are delicious as an hors d'oeuvre with drinks, but for something more substantial you could make the tart on sheets of puff pastry, slice it into eight squares, and serve a tossed green salad alongside.

Makes about 20 tarts

2	tablespoons extra-virgin olive oil
2	red or yellow onions, sliced ¼ inch thick
2	sheets store-bought frozen puff pastry
	About 1 cup creamy blue cheese, such as Cambozola or Cabrales
½	cup grated Parmesan cheese

Preheat the oven to 350°F.

In a large sauté pan, heat the olive oil over medium-high heat, then lower the heat to medium-low. Working in batches so as not to overcrowd the pan, add the onions and sauté until golden brown, about 10 minutes.

Use a cookie cutter to cut the puff pastry into 2-inch rounds. Place the rounds on a nonstick baking sheet. Using a smaller cutter, make an indentation along the edges of the pastry rounds to make a border; do not cut all the way through. Prick the center with a fork.

Place a teaspoon of blue cheese in the center of the pastry and top with some of the sauteed onion. Sprinkle with Parmesan cheese.

Place in the oven and bake for about 10 minutes, or until the pastry puffs up and the cheese turns golden. Serve immediately.

TURKISH EGGPLANT AND YOGURT SALAD

This salad is frequently served as part of mezze in Turkish homes, but can be equally satisfying as a main course for lunch or a light dinner.

Serves 8 as a side

2	tablespoons extra-virgin olive oil
2	large eggplants, cut into ¼ inch dice
2	whole cloves garlic, peeled
	Salt
2	(6-ounce) cans good-quality diced tomatoes, strained
2	cups Greek yogurt
4	cloves garlic, finely chopped
½	cup chopped fresh flat-leaf parsley

In a large sauté pan, heat the olive oil over medium-low heat. Add the eggplant and whole garlic cloves and cook until the eggplant is very soft, about 20 minutes. Season with a pinch of salt. Spoon the cooked eggplant into a decorative shallow platter. Top with the tomatoes and cool to room temperature.

In a medium bowl, mix together the yogurt and chopped garlic and season with salt. Spread over the eggplant and tomato. Sprinkle with the parsley to garnish and refrigerate until ready to serve. The salad should be served very cold.

Champagne and Pink Grapefruit Cocktail;
Blue Cheese and Caramelized Onion Tarts

PARSLEY AND WALNUT SALAD

Victoria was inspired to make this delicious salad after encountering a similar version in a restaurant in Istanbul.

Serves 8 as a side

5	cups roughly chopped fresh flat-leaf parsley
1	cup roughly chopped walnuts
6	scallions, white and green parts, thinly sliced
6	tablespoons extra-virgin olive oil
	Juice of 1 lemon
	Salt

In a salad bowl, toss together the parsley, walnuts, and scallions.

In a separate small bowl, whisk the olive oil with the lemon juice. Season with salt.

Just before serving, toss the parsley mixture with the dressing.

SHRIMP SKEWERS WITH CUMIN AND HONEY

These delicious lightly marinated skewers can work just as well with chicken.

Serves 8

2	tablespoons extra-virgin olive oil
	Juice of 1 lemon
	Juice of 1 orange
¼	cup honey
2½	tablespoons ground cumin
½	teaspoon salt, plus more to taste
24	large shrimp, peeled and deveined

Soak 8 wooden skewers in water for 30 minutes and set aside.

In a large bowl, whisk together the olive oil, lemon juice, orange juice, honey, cumin, and salt. Add the shrimp and marinate for about 20 minutes (do not overmarinate).

Preheat the oven to 400°F.

Place 3 shrimp on each skewer and arrange the skewers in a single layer on a baking sheet. Bake for 8 minutes, or until pink and cooked through. Transfer to a decorative platter and serve.

CHOCOLATE AND ALMOND CAKE

This simple, four-ingredient confection is not as caloric as other flour-based chocolate cakes, but it is just as delicious.

Serves 8

2	cups dark chocolate chips
5	extra-large eggs, separated
1	cup powdered sugar, plus more for dusting
1	cup ground almonds

Preheat the oven to 350°F and butter a 9-inch springform pan.

Melt the chocolate in a double boiler over simmering water until smooth.

In a large bowl, beat the egg yolks and powdered sugar with an electric mixer until pale in color and doubled in volume. In a separate bowl, beat the egg whites until stiff.

Using a spatula, add the ground almonds to the egg and sugar mixture, then stir the melted chocolate into the mixture. Fold in the egg whites in 2 batches and pour into the prepared pan.

Place in the oven and bake for about 20 minutes, or until the edges begin to separate from the pan and the center is just jiggly. The cake will finish cooking as it cools.

Place on a wire rack and cool completely, about 1 hour. Remove the cake from the pan, transfer to a decorative plate, and dust with powdered sugar.

Opposite: Shrimp Skewers with Cumin and Honey. Top: Orange and Red Onion Salad; Parsley and Walnut Salad, Turkish Eggplant and Yogurt Salad, Shrimp Skewers. Bottom: Chocolate and Almond Cake

CHILD'S PLAY
MARY AND MARK FREITAS

MARY FREITAS HAS FOND RECOLLECTIONS of her birthday parties as a child growing up in West Palm Beach. "A party was always a special occasion," she says. "All the children looked forward to it and loved to get dressed up. I remember being on a pony, in a dress."

Those innocent childhood moments are so indelible in her mind that they now inform her parties for her own children. For son Jack's second birthday celebration, she eschewed the usual Spiderman and pirate themes in favor of something a bit more old-fashioned.

"I wanted it to be sweet and childlike," she says as she arranges a "Happy Birthday, Jack" banner on the ficus hedge, "like the parties we had when we were growing up. Children just want to be children. Not everything needs to be commercialized."

Her vintage theme begins with the setting—the lawn of the Freitas family's Palm Beach home, where she has set up a play area with a tot-sized tent, toys, and the requisite little red wagons. On the other side of the pool sits a table and chairs "in miniature," decorated with balloon topiaries, pinwheel lollipops, simple garden bouquets, and melamine plates, all in Candy Land hues.

Because young children need some structure, she has hired a music instructor to lead sing-alongs and dances. As the kids play, the mommies watch and encourage, stopping every so often to enjoy some of Mary's homemade punch, a recipe that has been in her family for generations.

Though she and husband Mark have a personal chef, Mary does enjoy baking; she finds it creative and relaxing. Just as her mother used to do for her own birthday parties, she has baked the vanilla cupcakes and frosted "J" and "2" cookies for Jack and his friends.

Don't overwhelm your guests! Young children just like to play. A magician or something similar would be overwhelming. The less complicated the better.

Keep everything mini, from the table and chairs to the food portions to the silverware. Make sure everything is appropriate for little fingers.

Keep sugar to a minimum. Cake, and possibly cookies, is plenty. Avoid candy and other sweets, which can make children hyperactive.

Children love flowers, too. We have fresh flowers delivered every week, so I couldn't imagine a children's party without them. Keep them simple, bright, and not too fragrant for young guests.

When entertaining children, it's important to provide structure. You have to have a "script," but still let them loose within that framework.

The rest of the menu revolves around "surefire pleasers"—grilled cheese sandwiches cut into fun shapes, baked sweet potato fries, heart- and flower-shaped melon nuggets, a kid version of pigs in a blanket, and, of course, chicken fingers. "Everything was made with wholesome, identifiable ingredients," she says. "Nutritious, but yummy."

Like proper little young ladies and gentlemen, the guests sit around the pint-size table and enjoy lunch—for about ten minutes. The astute hostess has foreseen the set-in of ennui and has planned for it. In the nick of time, the bubble machine materializes and the guests are riveted as tiny, iridescent orbs float by.

As the celebration reaches its crescendo, the children discover the little red wagons. The older ones pull the younger ones, and Miss Angela, the music instructor, steps in to lead an impromptu parade. Shrieks and laughter animate the lazy Palm Beach afternoon.

Mary smiles as the sweet scene unfolds. It is exactly the way she envisioned it.

Please join us as we

celebrate

Jack's 2nd Birthday

Sunday August 14

4:00 pm

at our home

Palm Beach, Florida

Mary and Mark Freitas

...ck is
...hing 2!

PALM BEACH PARTY PUNCH

This nonalcoholic punch is enjoyed by adults and children alike. For an adult version, substitute Champagne for the ginger ale.

Makes 12 cups

- 1 (6-ounce) can frozen lemonade concentrate, thawed
- 1 (6-ounce) can frozen limeade concentrate, thawed
- 1 (46-ounce) can pineapple juice
- 1 (2-liter) bottle ginger ale

In a large punch bowl, combine the juice concentrates and pineapple juice. Refrigerate for 6 hours. To serve, add the ginger ale, stir, and ladle into glasses.

CRISP SUGAR COOKIES

A wonderful "go-to" cookie recipe for any occasion, from Christmas to bake sales. You make the dough ahead and let it rest overnight. If you'd like to frost them, use the buttercream frosting on page 40 or your favorite frosting recipe.

Makes 3 to 4 dozen cookies, depending upon the shape and size of the cutter

- 2 cups all-purpose flour, plus more for rolling the dough
- 1 teaspoon baking powder
- ½ teaspoon salt
- ¼ cup milk
- ½ teaspoon lemon extract
- ½ cup (1 stick) unsalted butter, at room temperature, plus more for buttering the cookie sheet
- 1 cup sugar
- 1 large egg

Sift the flour, baking powder, and salt into a large bowl. In a separate bowl, combine the milk and lemon extract.

In another bowl using an electric mixer, beat the butter with the sugar. Add the egg, then add the flour mixture, alternating with the milk mixture, in 2 additions. Mix well. Wrap the dough in plastic and refrigerate overnight.

Preheat the oven to 400°F. Butter 2 cookie sheets.

Roll the dough on a floured board to a ¼-inch thickness. Cut into desired shapes and transfer to the prepared cookie sheet.

Place in the oven and bake for 7 to 10 minutes, or until the cookies are lightly golden. Transfer to a wire rack to cool completely before serving.

VANILLA CUPCAKES

These yummy cupcakes are sure to be gobbled up by kids of all ages. We chose to top our cupcakes with a traditional buttercream frosting, but chocolate works just as well.

Makes 24 cupcakes

2½	cups all-purpose flour
2	teaspoons baking powder
½	teaspoon baking soda
½	teaspoon salt
½	cup milk
½	cup vegetable oil
1	teaspoon vanilla extract
½	cup (1 stick) unsalted butter, at room temperature
1	cup sugar
3	large eggs
	Traditional Buttercream Frosting (recipe follows)

Preheat the oven to 350°F and line 24 muffin cups with paper liners.

In a medium bowl, mix together the flour, baking powder, baking soda, and salt. In a separate bowl, combine the milk, oil, and vanilla.

In another bowl using an electric mixer set on high, beat the butter with the sugar until light and fluffy. Add the eggs, one at a time, beating well between each addition. Lower the speed of the mixer and add the flour mixture, alternating with the milk mixture and ending with the flour mixture, in 2 additions. Do not overmix.

Divide the batter among the 24 lined cups, filling each about two thirds full.

Place in the oven and bake for 15 to 20 minutes, or until a toothpick inserted in the center of a cupcake comes out clean. Transfer to a wire rack to cool completely, then use a spatula or butter knife to frost the cupcakes with the buttercream frosting.

TRADITIONAL BUTTERCREAM FROSTING
Makes 3 cups

½	cup (1 stick) unsalted butter, at room temperature
3¾	cups powdered sugar, sifted
3	to 4 tablespoons milk
2	teaspoons vanilla extract

In a large bowl using an electric mixer set on high, beat the butter until light and fluffy. Lower the speed and add the powdered sugar, 3 tablespoons of milk, and the vanilla. Increase the mixer speed to high and beat until fluffy, adding more milk to the frosting if it is too thick. The frosting can be stored in the refrigerator overnight. Bring to room temperature before using.

MOROCCAN HOSPITALITY
CLAUDE DASTE ROSINSKY

TO ENTER THE HOME OF Claude Daste Rosinsky is to be transported to the orange blossom–scented courtyards in Marrakech's medina. Not only was the home designed (in 1927, by Marion Sims Wyeth) with distinct Moorish accents, it has evolved into a showplace for art, antiques, and objects from Claude's native Morocco.

Born to French parents in Rabat, she grew up immersed in Moroccan culture. One of her most vivid memories is the scent of cumin, cinnamon, and fragrant waters wafting from her family's kitchen. At the time, it was considered inappropriate for expatriates to enter their own kitchens, let alone cook. The young Claude would sometimes crack the door and watch the cooks prepare the daily meals.

"I remember them working with vegetables and fruits that were so exquisite, and preparing the most amazing dishes," she says. "I was enchanted. I thought this was how everybody ate."

She got a rude awakening when she married. Her husband, Harold, asked her to cook something, and she, clueless as to the culinary arts, went out and bought the cookbook *Masterpieces of French Cuisine*, which included all the scrumptious, if complicated, dishes made by her family's chefs.

She slid the cookbook toward him and confidently announced, "Choose anything, and I will make it."

He chose a soufflé.

"Needless to say, it was a disaster," she says. "Harold told me, 'If you want to do a thing right, do it every day for a week.' So I did." She adds in an exuberant French accent, "Today, I am the queen of the soufflé."

Entertaining in the Moroccan tradition is her passion. A Moroccan-style dinner or lunch allows her to expose guests to her culture and showcase her collected objects, which include antique camel-bone tagines, hammered metal lanterns, embroidered textiles, and hand-painted earthenware that harmonize beautifully with European antiques and art.

For this late-spring lunch, Claude has recreated a traditional Moroccan summer feast. As her friends arrive, two young men in djellabas and fezes offer small glasses of almond milk and dates. In the riads of affluent families, it is traditional to welcome visitors this way.

Guests proceed through the courtyard to the cabana, which has been transformed for the occasion into an exquisite dining pavilion. Claude designed the table around an unusual centerpiece—a wrought-iron chandelier decked out with palms, orchids, heliconias, anthuriums, and bougainvilleas. The hanging centerpiece provides a central focus without obstructing any guest's view of the others.

Nothing on the table is too matched or too precious. Claude wanted it to look like it came together organically. A turquoise satin tablecloth topped with Venetian lace makes all the elements pop. Each place setting features a different hand-painted glass plate from a mixed-and-matched set Claude bought in Marrakech.

Even the smallest object has a story to tell. When the servers bring out the trays of mint tea, someone comments about the cozy on the teapot handle. As the hostess explains it, "These are folksy replicas of the Senegalese guards in front of the royal palace," where her father, the private physician to Sultan Mohammed V and, later, King Hassan, often worked. "It is my memory from when I was young."

It is those memories and experiences that she shares with friends when she entertains. And they are charmed by it. "I love to share with my guests different cultures and tastes and music," she says, "so we can enjoy the adventures we've all had traveling."

MENU FOR EIGHT

ALMOND-FLAVORED MILK

DATES

EGGPLANT RABAT STYLE

AVOCADO AND SHRIMP SALAD

CARROT AND RAISIN SALAD

TOMATO AND GREEN PEPPER SALAD, FEZ STYLE

CUCUMBER SALAD

BISTEEYA

TAGINE OF VEAL WITH ARTICHOKES

STRIPED BASS WITH SHRIMP

MOROCCAN RACK OF LAMB WITH BABY VEGETABLES

FRUIT SALAD

BRIOUTS

MINT TEA

PREPARED BY CHEF RACHID ROUIJEL

ALMOND-FLAVORED MILK

A wonderful welcome drink, serve in decorative cordial glasses.

Serves 8

16	ounces (3½ to 4 cups) blanched almonds
1	cup sugar
2	tablespoons rosewater
2	cups milk

In a food processor, grind the almonds and sugar until very fine. Add the rosewater and 1 cup of water and process to a smooth paste. Add 1 cup of milk, continue to process, then add another cup of water and process again. Add the last cup of milk and process for a few seconds more. Pass through a very fine sieve into a bowl, pressing with the back of a spoon to extract as much liquid as possible. Refrigerate until ready to serve.

To serve, pour into small shot or cordial glasses.

EGGPLANT RABAT STYLE

It takes a while to make the eggplant a divine golden mahogany color, caramelized and aromatic, but the results are worth it!

Serves 8

2	large eggplants
2	large cloves garlic, slivered
¼	cup extra-virgin olive oil
	Juice of 1 lemon
¼	cup chopped fresh flat-leaf parsley
¼	cup chopped fresh cilantro (optional)
1	teaspoon paprika
1	teaspoon ground cumin
	Salt
1	pint grape tomatoes, sliced, for garnish

Clockwise from top:
Avocado and Shrimp Salad,
Cucumber Salad, and
Carrot and Raisin Salad

Preheat the oven to 400°F.

Working with a sharp paring knife, make slits in the eggplant and push a sliver of garlic into each slit. Place the eggplant in the oven on their sides and bake until the skin is charred and the flesh is very soft. Remove from the oven and set aside to cool.

When the eggplant is cool enough to handle, peel the skin off and transfer the flesh to a strainer to drain all the bitter juices. Mash or finely chop the eggplant flesh and roasted garlic.

In a medium bowl, whisk together the olive oil, lemon juice, parsley, cilantro, if using, paprika, and cumin. Season with salt and add to the eggplant mixture.

Place the eggplant mixture in a large skillet over medium-high heat and cook, pressing down with a slotted spatula to release all the juices, until it is mahogany brown and thickened to a spreadable consistency, 20 to 30 minutes.

Transfer to a serving bowl and garnish with sliced baby tomatoes. Serve warm or at room temperature.

TOMATO AND GREEN PEPPER SALAD, FEZ STYLE

Guests will love the complex flavors of this very easy-to-make salad. Don't worry if those bits of charred green peppers make it into the salad bowl—it gives the salad a fabulous authenticity and great depth of flavor!

Serves 8

4	large green bell peppers
4	large tomatoes
2	tablespoons extra-virgin olive oil
	Juice of 1 lemon
2	large cloves garlic, crushed
½	teaspoon sweet paprika
¼	teaspoon ground cumin
	Salt and freshly ground black pepper
1	large preserved lemon

Preheat the oven to 450°F.

Place the peppers on an ungreased baking sheet and bake for 10 minutes. Turn peppers over and continue to bake 10 minutes more, or until peppers are charred on all sides. Place the blackened peppers under a towel and set aside to cool.

When cool, remove the skins and seeds and dice the peppers. Place in a decorative glass bowl.

Bring a small saucepan of water to a boil. Cut a cross in the bottom of each tomato and immerse in the boiling water for about 15 seconds; the skins should slide off. Slice the tomatoes in half and squeeze some of their juices; discard the juice. Dice the tomatoes and add to the green peppers.

In a small bowl, whisk together the olive oil, lemon juice, garlic, paprika, and cumin. Season with salt and pepper. Pour over the prepared vegetables and mix well.

Rinse the preserved lemon and cut away the pulp. Cut the peel into slivers and sprinkle over the salad. Serve at room temperature.

Top: Mint Tea; Bottom: Almond Milk and Dates

TAGINE OF VEAL WITH ARTICHOKES

Canned artichokes are easy to find year-round, but of course you can use fresh wild artichokes or baby artichokes available in the spring. You'll need 8 pounds, rinsed and trimmed—don't be afraid of the large amount, as once they are trimmed they will shrink to almost nothing.

Serves 8

	Salt
4	pieces (approximately 4 pounds) veal shank
¼	cup extra-virgin olive oil
2	tablespoons finely chopped fresh ginger
2	tablespoons saffron, crushed
5	(4-ounce cans) artichoke hearts, rinsed
	Rind of 1 large preserved lemon, rinsed
½	cup olives, pitted
	Freshly ground black pepper

Salt the veal. In a large pot, heat the olive oil over medium-high heat. Brown the meat on both sides until golden, then add the ginger and saffron and enough water to cover the meat about halfway. Bring to a boil, then cover, lower the heat, and simmer until most of the liquid evaporates and the meat falls easily from the bone, about 2 hours.

Using a slotted spoon, remove the meat and roughly chop into large pieces. Add the artichokes, lemon rind, and olives to the pan and simmer until soft, 20 to 25 minutes. Crush a couple of artichokes to thicken the sauce. Return the meat to the pan to heat through, season with salt and pepper, and serve hot.

STRIPED BASS WITH SHRIMP

This wonderful combination of ingredients doesn't compete with the delicate flavor of the bass. For another occasion, serve this with a bowl of couscous to mop up all the delicious juices.

Serves 8

1	whole striped bass (about 6 pounds), cleaned
	Salt and freshly ground pepper
1	cup extra-virgin olive oil
4	large tomatoes, peeled and diced
3	large onions, diced
2	large green bell peppers, diced
2	whole heads garlic, peeled and crushed
1	tablespoon saffron
1	pound shrimp, peeled, deveined and cooked
¼	cup fresh flat-leaf parsley leaves, for garnish
5	yellow and orange bell peppers, roasted, for garnish (optional).

Preheat the oven to 350°F.

Season the striped bass with salt and pepper.

In a large saucepan, warm ²⁄₃ cup of the olive oil over medium-low heat. Add the tomatoes, onions, green peppers, garlic, and saffron. Season with salt and pepper. Bring to a simmer and cook until all the ingredients are softened, about 15 minutes. Remove from the heat and cool.

Use about half the mixture to stuff inside the fish. Add the remaining ¹⁄₃ cup olive oil in a large pan and put the fish in the pan. Place in the oven and bake for 30 to 40 minutes, until the fish is cooked through.

To serve, gently reheat the reserved vegetable mixture with the shrimp and spoon over the fish. Garnish with the parsley leaves. If using, arrange roasted yellow and orange peppers around platter to add a punch of color to presentation.

BISTEEYA

Bisteeya is a traditional Moroccan pie made with phyllo dough and filled with a mixture of squab, almonds, and cinnamon. Our bisteeya substitutes squab for breasts of chicken. It is a truly delicious mixture of sweet and spicy flavors.

Serves 8

3	tablespoons extra-virgin olive oil
5	chicken breast cutlets, cubed
	Salt and freshly ground black pepper
4	cloves garlic, sliced
4	tablespoons unsalted butter, plus 4 tablespoons melted butter to brush the phyllo sheets
1	cup diced onion
2	tablespoons all-purpose flour
½	cup lemon juice
1½	cups chicken broth, preferably low-sodium
2	large egg yolks
1	tablespoon finely chopped preserved lemon
1	cup sliced almonds
1	tablespoon granulated sugar
8	sheets phyllo dough, plus 1 or 2 more if needed
1	tablespoon ground cinnamon
1	tablespoon powdered sugar

Preheat the oven to 375°F.

Heat the olive oil in a large sauté pan over medium heat. Season the chicken with salt and pepper; add the chicken and garlic to the pan and cook, stirring often so as not to brown the pieces, until the chicken is just cooked through, 8 to 10 minutes. Remove from the heat and set aside.

Wipe out the pan and add 2 tablespoons of the butter. Place over medium heat and melt the butter; add the onions and sauté until translucent, about 5 to 7 minutes. Stir in the flour and cook until it dissolves. Stir in the lemon juice and chicken broth and bring just to a boil. Lower the heat and simmer until the sauce thickens, 3 to 5 minutes. Stir in the egg yolks and allow to cook until the egg curdles, then stir in the chicken and preserved lemon. Season with salt and pepper. Remove from the heat and set aside to cool.

Melt 1 tablespoon of the remaining butter in a small saucepan over medium heat; add the almonds and granulated sugar and cook until the almonds turn golden, about 30 seconds. Keep an eye on this as it goes from golden brown and delicious to burnt in seconds. Remove from the heat and add to the chicken mixture.

Butter a 9-inch round oven dish and place 1 sheet of phyllo on the bottom of the dish; brush with melted butter. Overlap the remaining phyllo sheets, brushing each with melted butter, to cover the dish completely, leaving plenty of dough over the edges.

Fill the dish with the chicken-almond mixture and fold the overlapping phyllo sheets over the mixture. Brush with melted butter and add sheets to the top, if needed. Brush with melted butter again and pour any remaining melted butter around the pie.

Place in the oven and bake for 40 minutes, or until the top is golden.

Remove from the oven and, using oven mitts, invert the pie onto a decorative plate. Sprinkle with cinnamon and powdered sugar and serve.

Briouts;
Opposite: Bisteeya

EN PLEIN AIR
PERFECT OUTDOOR GATHERINGS

IN THE FRENCH TRADITION
ANNIE AND MICHAEL FALK

ANNIE FALK LIKES TO TELL, with a combination of humor and self-effacement, a story about the summer she learned to cook. She was in the south of France, under the tutelage of Roger Vergé, attempting to absorb from the master some culinary adroitness that would serve her in her new marriage and help her perfect the art of entertaining.

Problem was, she didn't even know how to crack an egg.

"It was like walking into calculus class without ever having taken math," she says.

It didn't take long for Vergé to lose patience with her. When she asked one time too many about the difference between rosemary and thyme, he told her that if she ever wanted to walk into his kitchen again, she would have to wake up at an ungodly hour and go with him to the market.

Not one to argue with a Frenchman wielding a chef's knife, she did it. And it was the best thing that could have happened to her. "Following the food from the market to the kitchen made a huge difference," she says. "To this day, this is how I shop and how I cook."

The story rings especially true on a morning when Annie and daughter Gigi scour the local green market for fresh produce—and inspiration. They find gorgeous eggplant, heirloom tomatoes just plucked from the vine, fragrant berries, and "truckloads" of fleshy avocados. Ideas swirl in Annie's mind, and she begins to formulate the menu for a dinner party she and husband Michael are giving later that week.

"I let the ingredients dictate the menu, rather than the other way around," she says.

Armed with this bounty of seasonal produce, she decides on a chilled avocado soup, vegetables Provençal, watercress salad with goat cheese toasts, and a frozen raspberry soufflé, along with a main course of lamb Orientale rolled with garden vegetables. Many of the dishes are based on classic Vergé recipes that she has simplified and tweaked into her own version of "cuisine of the sun," and further refined with input from local French chef Thierry Miroir, who is helping her prepare the dinner.

The veggies are organic, sustainable, and locally sourced; the lamb is hormone-free and humanely raised. The Falks have been eating this way since before it was fashionable. They believe in wholesome food that does not unnecessarily tax the planet's resources, be it for everyday meals or for entertaining.

Greeting guests with a specialty cocktail is always fun and a great conversation starter, but be sure to have red and white wines available, too. Serve sparkling water in the same tumbler or wine glass other guests are drinking from; this way guests who are not indulging feel at ease.

Decorating should not be confined to the dinner table. Flowers, candles, and whimsical objects can all be used to create a sense of warmth and ambiance throughout your home, including the powder room.

Whether you choose to decorate your table with flowers, objects, or candles, there is one rule to remember: Centerpieces should be below eye level or thin and clear. No one likes to dodge an enormous centerpiece to talk to their dinner partners. Save tall arrangements for the entryway.

When entertaining a party of six or more, always use place cards. When guests know where they are sitting, it puts them at ease immediately and they are assured you have given thoughtful consideration as to who their dinner partner will be.

Dinner is served outdoors under a pergola on which grows a rare jade vine. The vine blooms once a year around Easter, signaling to Annie that it is time for a final round of intimate dinner parties with good friends before they all retreat to their summer homes.

The table is set with ceramic dishes hand-painted in a palette of browns and blues, which the Falks had custom made during a trip to Italy, along with amber glass goblets, vintage glass-covered dishes, and mercury glass votives. A tropical floral arrangement in a long glass vessel adds jewel-toned pops of color, as well as a modern counterpoint to the vintage elements.

A second table is set in the courtyard. Because the Falks feel strongly about including their teenage daughters in all they do—their travels, their philanthropic endeavors, and even their parties—they have invited them and their friends to hold their own mini gathering. The girls' table is a kaleidoscope of green, pink, and purple hues, with fun elements such as bandana napkins and a candy centerpiece that Annie herself made.

As friends enjoy dinner and lively conversation under the vine-festooned pergola, one raves about the raspberry soufflé and asks Annie whether she made it.

"Yes," she smiles. "I did."

Roger Vergé would be proud.

CHILLED AVOCADO SOUP

This is a delicious, simple-to-make soup that gathers all its attention in the decorative aspect: The colors are wonderful, the texture velvety smooth. If condiment squeeze bottles are not in your kitchen, serve the soup garnished with a dollop of crème fraîche and slivers of roasted red pepper. This recipe calls for Espellete pepper, a variety of a chili pepper grown in the Basque region where it is integral to the cuisine.

Serves 6

3	avocados, peeled, pitted, and roughly chopped
6	cups milk
	Espellete pepper
1½	tablespoons lemon juice
	Salt and freshly ground black pepper
3	tablespoons crème fraîche or sour cream
2	jarred roasted red peppers
2	medium baguettes, each cut into 16 thin slices
4	to 6 tablespoons extra-virgin olive oil
	Hazelnut oil (optional)

Working in batches, puree the avocados in a blender with the milk, Espellete pepper to taste, and lemon juice. Season with salt and pepper. Pour into a container and chill until ready to serve, at least 2 or 3 hours.

Spoon the crème fraîche into a condiment squeeze bottle. Puree the red peppers in the blender and spoon into another condiment squeeze bottle.

Brush the baguette slices with the olive oil and toast until golden. Drain excess oil on paper towels and set aside.

To serve, ladle the soup into bowls or soup plates. Alternating between the crème fraîche and the roasted red pepper puree, decorate the soup by drawing circles, beginning in the center with a small circle and keeping the spacing between the circles as even as possible. Using a skewer or wooden toothpick, "cut" the circles by drawing 6 to 8 lines from the outer circle to the center circle to make the design. Garnish with a drop of hazelnut oil, if using, in the center. Serve with the toasted baguette slices.

LAMB ORIENTALE WITH SPINACH, CARROTS, AND AFGHAN SAUCE

This colorful dish makes for a striking presentation and combines beautifully with the exotic flavor profile of the Afghan sauce. Annie makes this dish with farm-raised, hormone-free lamb.

Serves 6

½	pound frozen spinach, thawed and squeezed dry
	Salt and freshly ground black pepper
2	tablespoons unsalted butter, cut into small pieces
½	pound carrots, shredded
3	pounds lamb leg shank, deboned
3	tablespoons extra-virgin olive oil
	Afghan Sauce (recipe follows)

Spread the spinach over a 10 x 15-inch piece of plastic wrap and flatten it with your hands. Season with salt and pepper and dot with the butter. Spread the carrots on top. Working as if it were a jelly roll, and using the plastic wrap as a guide, roll the carrots and spinach to make a tight roll the approximate size of the lamb shank bone. Wrap in the plastic and freeze overnight.

Preheat the oven to 350°F.

Remove the plastic wrap from the frozen spinach-carrot roll. Carefully insert the roll in the lamb shank (where the bone was removed) and place on a baking sheet. Drizzle with the olive oil and season with salt and pepper.

Place in the oven and cook for about 45 minutes, or until the lamb is cooked through. Let rest for about 10 minutes and slice.

To serve, ladle half the Afghan sauce on the bottom of a serving platter. Arrange the sliced lamb on top and pass the remaining sauce at the table.

AFGHAN SAUCE

Makes about 4 cups

4	tablespoons (½ stick) unsalted butter
1	pound shallots, sliced
2	cups chicken broth, preferably low-sodium
2	cups beef broth, preferably low-sodium
1	(28-ounce) can crushed or pureed tomatoes
½	teaspoon ground cardamom
½	teaspoon ground cumin
½	teaspoon ground turmeric
½	teaspoon ground cinnamon
¼	teaspoon ground cayenne
	Salt and freshly ground black pepper
½	cup plain whole-milk yogurt

In a stockpot, heat the butter over medium heat. Add the shallots and sauté until just softened, 5 to 7 minutes. Add the chicken broth, beef broth, tomatoes, cardamom, cumin, turmeric, cinnamon, and cayenne and season with salt and pepper. Bring to a boil, then reduce the heat and simmer until most of the liquid has evaporated, about 45 minutes.

Working in batches, puree in a blender. Taste and adjust the seasoning. Return to the pot, add the yogurt, and keep warm over low heat until ready to serve.

VEGETABLES PROVENÇAL

Although jalapeño is not a typical Provençal ingredient, it gives these delicious roasted vegetables a wonderful smokiness and depth of flavor. Slice or cube all the vegetables to an even size to assure a prettier presentation and even cooking times.

Serves 6

1	cup extra-virgin olive oil
1	large eggplant, sliced
2	medium zucchini, sliced
1	large red bell pepper, cored, seeded, and sliced
1	large green bell pepper, cored, seeded, and sliced
1	large red onion, sliced
1	large yellow onion, sliced
2	large tomatoes, sliced
1	head garlic, peeled
2	tablespoons finely chopped fresh flat-leaf parsley
2	tablespoons finely chopped fresh tarragon
2	tablespoons finely chopped fresh thyme
2	tablespoons finely chopped fresh rosemary
1	tablespoon finely chopped fresh marjoram
1	jalapeño pepper, seeded and sliced
	Salt and freshly ground black pepper
1	sprig fresh rosemary or thyme for garnish (optional)

Top Right: Vegetables Provençal; Bottom: Lamb Orientale with Spinach, Carrots, and Afghan Sauce, and Couscous with Pine Nuts

Preheat the oven to 450°F.

Pour ½ cup of the olive oil into a roasting pan and add the eggplant, zucchini, bell peppers, onions, tomatoes, and garlic.

In a medium bowl, combine the parsley, tarragon, thyme, rosemary, marjoram, and jalapeño. Whisk in the remaining ½ cup of olive oil and pour the mixture over the vegetables. Season with salt and pepper.

Cover with aluminum foil, place in the oven, and bake for 1 hour, or until the vegetables are soft and cooked through. Remove the foil from the vegetables, stir gently, and return to the oven for 10 minutes for the vegetables to crisp slightly.

To serve, transfer to a decorative dish, season with salt and pepper, and garnish with a sprig of rosemary, if using.

FROZEN RASPBERRY SOUFFLÉ

The recipe calls for raspberries, but any fresh, seasonal berry can be substituted with equally delicious results. It's a fabulous freeze-ahead dessert.

Serves 6

1	pint raspberries
⅔	cup superfine sugar
⅔	cup water
4	large egg whites
	Pinch of salt
1	cup crème fraîche, chilled
2	tablespoons unsweetened cocoa powder
	Fresh mint, for garnish (optional)

Set a few raspberries aside for decorating and place the remaining berries in a blender and puree. Strain the puree through a fine-mesh sieve set over a bowl, pressing on it with a spoon to extract all the juice; discard the seeds. Cover and refrigerate.

Combine the superfine sugar and water in a small stainless steel saucepan, place over high heat, and heat until it begins to bubble. Place a candy thermometer in the saucepan. When the sugar syrup reaches a temperature of 234° to 238°F, remove from the heat. If you don't have a candy thermometer, keep a small bowl of ice water on the side, and when the syrup is bubbling vigorously (3 to 5 minutes), drop a bit into the ice water. If you can gather it into a soft ball, it is ready.

Place the egg whites in a large bowl and add the salt. Beat with an electric mixer, beginning on low speed and gradually increasing to high, until stiff peaks form. Reduce the speed of the mixer to low and pour a thin, steady stream of the syrup into the egg whites, continuing to beat at low speed and turning the bowl until the mixture has cooled. Cover and refrigerate.

Place the crème fraîche in a bowl and beat with an electric mixer until whipped. Return to the refrigerator.

Cut waxed paper into 6 strips that are 2½ inches wide by 12 inches long. Wrap a strip around the outside of six 6-ounce soufflé molds and secure with a rubber band or tape, forming a raised collar extending about an inch above the mold. Place the molds in the refrigerator.

When the egg mixture is well chilled, remove all the ingredients from the refrigerator. Fold half the fruit puree into the egg mixture, blending well. Fold the remaining fruit puree into the whipped crème fraîche with a wooden spoon. Then fold the two mixtures together. Divide the mixture among the 6 chilled soufflé molds, cover, and freeze for 5 to 6 hours or overnight.

About 20 to 30 minutes before serving, remove the soufflés from the freezer and place in the refrigerator. Just before serving, remove the collars and sift cocoa powder on top of each soufflé. Decorate with the reserved berries and fresh mint, if using.

Watercress Salad with Goat Cheese Toasts

Frozen Raspberry Soufflé

DINNER IN THE COUNTRY
KARIN AND JOE LUTER

WHEN THINKING OF PALM BEACH, quail fields, moss-draped oak hammocks, and fire pits seldom come to mind. But this, too, is Palm Beach—or, at least, the western version of it.

Karin and Joe Luter are among many Palm Beachers to flock to the western outpost of Okeechobee, seeking wide-open spaces, the solitude of the country, and outdoor pursuits such as horseback riding and wing shooting. Tonight the Luters have invited a group of new friends from town to their country home in Pine Creek Sporting Club. The evening is a kick-off for the Ultimate Dinner Party, a gathering of Palm Beach's savviest hosts, tastemakers, trendsetters, wine collectors, and culinary stars. The Luters are honoring the supporters of the charity it benefits, Children's Home Society of Florida.

Karin loves to host guests at home, regardless of where home is. "Entertaining at home is such a personal and self-expressive way to entertain," she says. "It's wonderful to be surrounded by favorite things and to invite people into your private world."

Every "home," of course, has its own character, and that is conveyed in the ambiance she sets. At Pine Creek, which is about an hour's drive from Palm Beach but a world apart, it's all about "nature, sport, and relaxed elegance."

A big part of the ambiance, Karin believes, is expressed through fashion. Known for her style sense, she is always appropriately dressed for the occasion, be it a grand gala or a poolside barbecue. It's not about formality; it's about honoring the setting and the circumstances. That was instilled in her at a young age.

"I still have a vintage photo of myself and my mother before a holiday party," she says. "She looked impeccable in her red pencil skirt and black stilettos. I always remember that, and how important it is to welcome your guests looking your best."

Tonight the occasion calls for dressing down, and guests arrive in everything from jeans and cashmere sweaters to informal dresses—all beautifully accessorized, of course. Drinks are taken at the "tree house"—a bar built of rough-hewn logs, wood planks, and thatch around a specimen oak tree. As guests sip the signature cocktail, the roar of an approaching helicopter pierces the tranquil dusk, announcing the arrival of the final guests.

When all have assembled, the group walks across the hammock to another old oak, beneath which the table has been set. The guests marvel at the magical scene set

Relax. It's just a party. If the hostess is having a good time, guests will too.

On the table, embroidered and monogrammed linens are classic and always appropriate. For monograms, I prefer tone on tone to contrasting colors.

Instead of single arrangements in the center of the table, try different floral presentations, such as multiple vessels with single flowers.

When entertaining in the country, bring something from the setting to the table. That's how you establish a sense of place.

I always stock the following: Parmigiano Reggiano, prosciutto, chocolate, Champagne, chamomile tea, and pigs in a blanket.

My cardinal rules for parties: People make the party; when seating, separate spouses; greet your guests with a warm, personal welcome and facilitate introductions; be specific on the invitation about the dress code; always keep white and rosé wine, and Champagne, well chilled, and do not overfill glasses.

by Luter. When designing the table, her style is subtle yet elegant, always taking a cue from the environment. For this outdoor party, up lights illuminate the textural bark of the oak tree, while oversized silver lanterns filled with pillar candles flicker above a teak table set with zebra-print runners, silver sculptures of game fowl, and reflective square vessels holding an assortment of white bulb flowers.

A blast of wind comes out of nowhere, and the hostess wearily eyes the gathering clouds. As the guests are seated, the first few drops are felt, and she makes a quick decision to have the table disassembled and reassembled inside.

Even the best-laid plans have to come with a Plan B.

In a matter of moments, just before a torrential downpour, the table is stripped of all objects and reset in the clubhouse under the gaze of mounted trophies. No one seems to mind the last-minute swap, focusing instead on the refined country cuisine, which includes a potpie filled with wild turkey shot earlier that week by NFL great Tucker Frederickson, a fellow club member.

As the storm rages outside, the environment inside is warm, the conversation is thought-provoking, and the laughter crackles like the logs in the fire. After all, the scene helps, but it's the people who make the celebration.

MENU FOR EIGHT

MEYERS'S MARK

CORNMEAL-CRUSTED QUAIL

GREENS FROM THE GARDEN WITH ROASTED BABY BEETS
AND
SEVENTY-FIVE-YEAR AGED BALSAMIC VINEGAR

WILD TURKEY POT PIE

GRILLED FLORIDA GROUPER WITH RAINBOW BABY CARROTS
AND GOAT CHEESE GRITS

PASTA PRIMAVERA WITH SPINACH, MARINATED YELLOW AND RED TOMATOES, ASPARAGUS, EGGPLANT, TRI-COLOR PEPPERS, AND PARMIGIANO REGGIANO

GORGONZOLA WITH ORANGE BLOSSOM HONEY, PECORINO ROMANO, AND AGED MANCHEGO WITH RED AND GREEN GRAPES, APPLE SLICES, STRAWBERRIES, BLUEBERRIES, ALMONDS, WALNUTS, AND PECANS

WHITE CHOCOLATE AND BLUEBERRY BREAD PUDDING

SELECTION OF COFFEE AND TEAS

PREPARED AND SELECTED BY PINE CREEK CLUB
EXECUTIVE CHEF CHRISTIAN WATSON

MEYERS'S MARK

This drink was created (and named) in honor of Pine Creek founder Steve Meyers. It's a favorite at the club.

Makes 1 drink

- 1 ounce Maker's Mark
- ½ ounce Myers's rum
- ½ cup unsweetened iced tea
- Splash of orange juice
- Splash of Grand Marnier
- Kumquat Simple Syrup (recipe follows) to taste
- Sliced kumquats for garnish

Mix the ingredients in a large glass, add ice, and serve garnished with sliced kumquats.

KUMQUAT SIMPLE SYRUP

Makes 1 cup

- 1 cup sugar
- 1 cup water
- ¼ cup fresh kumquat slices

In a medium saucepan, combine the sugar, water, and kumquat slices; place over medium-high heat and bring to a boil. Stir, reduce the heat, and simmer for 5 minutes, making sure the sugar is completely dissolved. Remove from the heat and allow to steep for 10 minutes. Cool, then cover and refrigerate to chill. Remove the kumquat slices and strain the simple syrup, discarding the kumquat pulp.

Top: Meyers's Mark;
Bottom: Wild Turkey Pot Pie

CORNMEAL-CRUSTED QUAIL

This is a tasty alternative to traditional Southern fried quail. Follow the recipe for a fabulous first course, but for a great hors d'oeuvre, cut into bite-size nuggets and serve with your favorite hot sauce.

Serves 8

1	cup cornmeal
⅓	cup rice flour
2	tablespoons sweet smoked paprika
4	whole quail, quartered, backbone removed, rinsed, and patted dry
	Salt and freshly ground black pepper
	Peanut oil for frying
1	tablespoon kosher salt
2	teaspoons cracked black pepper
8	ounces salad greens

In a small bowl, combine the cornmeal, rice flour, and smoked paprika.

Season both sides of the quail with salt and cracked black pepper and dredge in the cornmeal mixture.

Heat 1 inch of peanut oil in a deep medium skillet over medium-high heat until it reaches 350°F on a deep-frying thermometer.

Remove the quail legs from the seasoning, shaking off excess cornmeal. Carefully place the quail legs into the hot oil and fry, turning once, until deep golden brown, 3 to 4 minutes. With a slotted spoon, transfer the legs to paper towels to drain. Add the quail breasts to the hot oil and fry, turning once, until deep golden brown, about 3 minutes. With a slotted spoon, transfer the breasts to paper towels to drain. Allow to rest for a couple of minutes before serving. Serve over the greens.

WILD TURKEY POT PIE

Though delicious with wild turkey, this hearty dish can also be made with store-bought turkey, game fowl, or chicken.

Makes 1 pie; serves 8

4	tablespoons (½ stick) unsalted butter
1	large yellow onion, diced
½	cup diced carrot
½	cup diced celery
3	cloves garlic, diced
	Salt and freshly ground black pepper
2	tablespoons all-purpose flour
2	cups chicken broth, preferably low-sodium
3	tablespoons heavy cream
1½	pounds wild turkey breast, cooked and diced
16	ounces peas, thawed if frozen
3	tablespoons chopped fresh flat-leaf parsley
1½	tablespoons chopped fresh chives
1½	tablespoons chopped fresh thyme
1½	tablespoons chopped fresh sage
1	sheet frozen puff pastry, thawed
1	large egg, beaten

Preheat the oven to 350°F.

In a large sauté pan, melt the butter over medium heat. Add the onions, carrots, celery, and garlic and sauté until the onions are just translucent, 5 to 7 minutes. Season with salt and pepper. Add the flour and stir to combine well, making sure all the flour is absorbed and no longer white. Add the broth and cream, bring to a boil, then reduce the heat and simmer for 5 to 7 minutes to thicken. Add the turkey, peas, parsley, chives, thyme, and sage and mix well.

Transfer the turkey mixture to a 9 x 13-inch rectangular or 10-inch round oven-to-table decorative dish. Cover the dish with the puff pastry, closing the edges and making a decorative border with a fork. Place on a baking sheet.

In a small bowl, whisk the egg with 1 tablespoon of water and brush the top of the pastry with the egg wash. Place in the oven and bake for about 25 minutes, or until the pastry is golden brown and the filling is bubbling hot. Let rest for 5 minutes before serving.

Cornmeal-Crusted Quail

WHITE CHOCOLATE AND BLUEBERRY BREAD PUDDING

Starting this pudding a day ahead allows for the bread to soak up the delicious cream and egg mixture. Day-old bread is a must, as it gives the pudding a wonderful crispness that fresh bread doesn't achieve. Fresh blueberries, preferably wild, add a burst of flavor to this country dessert. We love it topped with homemade blueberry jam, but a store-bought jam will also do. You can also add a dollop of whipped cream, garnished with fresh mint leaves and slices of orange.

Serves 8

6	large eggs
3	cups heavy cream
1	cup milk
1¼	cups sugar
½	teaspoon vanilla extract
	Pinch of salt
1	loaf day-old ciabatta bread, cut into 1-inch cubes
3	ounces white chocolate, shaved or cut into small pieces
2	cups fresh blueberries
2	tablespoons orange zest, plus more for garnish
	Whipped cream for garnish

In a large bowl, whisk together the eggs, heavy cream, milk, and 1 cup of the sugar. Add the vanilla and salt.

Add the bread and mix well. Cover with plastic wrap and refrigerate for at least 12 hours.

Preheat the oven to 275°F and butter a 9 x 13-inch rectangular or 10-inch round oven-to-table baking dish.

Remove the bread mixture from the refrigerator and fold in the white chocolate, blueberries, and orange zest. Transfer to the prepared baking dish and cover with aluminum foil.

Place in the oven and bake for 1¾ hours. Remove the foil and sprinkle with the remaining ¼ cup of sugar. Raise the oven temperature to 500°F, return the pudding to the oven, and bake for 10 to 15 minutes, or until the top is golden. Serve warm, garnished with whipped cream and a touch of orange zest.

THE SEVENTH CHUKKER
NIC ROLDAN

POLO IS, BY ALL ACCOUNTS, a glamorous sport. From the beautiful, elite horses—and horsemen—pitted against each other in adrenaline-charged matches to the Champagne flowing field side, polo has earned its image as the "sport of kings."

But off the field, it's another story entirely. After a match, the players retreat to their barns to do what they love most: spend time with one another and with their horses away from the limelight, sharing good food and even better company.

"After polo matches, we get all the grooms and players together and fire up an *asado* at one of the barns," says Nic Roldan, seven-goaler who has become one of the most recognizable faces of the sport. "We do much more of that than we do the glitz and glamour. To us, this is very real and authentic to our Argentine roots."

The Argentine-born, American-raised Nic maintains the traditions of his homeland in every aspect of his lifestyle. When entertaining, he doesn't step outside his comfort zone. He hosts casual, down-to-earth barbecues with fellow polo players, like-minded friends, and family. The horses and dogs are never far away, either; they, too, are members of the family.

For this post-match gathering, Nic is hosting an asado, the Argentine version of a barbecue. In Argentina, where beef is both plentiful and flavorful, the asado is a veritable meat fest. It consists of a variety of meats, sausages, offal, and blood puddings slow cooked on a *parilla*, or grill, placed over a smoldering fire pit.

Though this is Wellington, Florida, not Argentina, the composition of the asado is highly authentic. The only difference is the addition of chicken, which Nic justifies thus: "I got it because there are girls coming."

As the *asadors* salt the meat and place it on the grill, Nic and his friends gather round the fire, sitting on hay bales topped with Argentine textiles, and share a few laughs as the sun's last rays paint the sky lavender and lion-gold. The host's father, Raul, with mate in

Keep it simple. All you need is the barbecue pit, a few hay bales, and some textiles for color. This is how they do it in the big estancias in Argentina.

Make sure you have a variety of meats (see recommended cuts). Not everyone likes ribs, or blood sausage, or organ meats. Know your guests and plan your menu according to what they like.

Don't overseason the meat. A little salt rubbed on both sides goes a long way.

Since an asado is served outdoors, bring in elements from nature. Wildflowers that are not too carefully arranged look beautiful on the table. I don't use place cards, but if you do, river stones or leaves (with names written with a Sharpie) work better than traditional paper.

hand, chats up the *asadors* and offers his two cents on how the skirt steak should be prepared.

Nic's mother and father are never missing from his parties. "We've always been a close family," he says. "We do everything together. No matter where I am in the world, my first call in the morning is to my mom and dad."

When the meat comes off the fire, the crowd gathers round the carving table. It is traditional in Argentina to carve the meat—often with one's own knife, called the *cuchilla*—just as it gets delivered from the grill, and to eat the first sizzling morsels with a piece of bread before sitting down at the table.

The group eventually does sit down at a long table beneath the pergola, sipping white sangria and feasting on the chargrilled meat, which is served simply with a green salad and bread. After dinner, a few guests retreat fireside, enjoying the warmth from the embers and the camaraderie as the night comes to a close.

Next week, there will be another match—and another opportunity to celebrate.

WHITE WINE SANGRIA

DEE ROLDAN'S BEEF EMPANADAS

MIXED GREEN SALAD WITH
GREEN APPLES AND WALNUTS

MIXED GRILL ASADO

FRESH BAKED BREAD

RAUL ROLDAN'S MATÉ

WHITE WINE SANGRIA

Made with Argentine or Spanish white wine and green fruit, this beverage is light and refreshing as a predinner cocktail.

Serves 8

1	bottle Spanish or Argentine white wine
¼	cup sugar
	Juice of ½ lime
1	lime, thinly sliced
	Juice of ½ lemon
1	lemon, thinly sliced
1	Granny Smith apple, thinly sliced
1½	cups seedless green grapes, sliced in half
1	cup apple juice
½	bunch mint leaves, finely torn
	Pinch of salt
12	ounces plain seltzer water
	Ice

In a large pitcher or mixing bowl, combine the wine and sugar and stir until the sugar dissolves. Add the remaining ingredients except the seltzer water. Mix well and let the sangria sit from 1½ to 4 hours in the refrigerator. Before serving, stir, then add the seltzer water and ice cubes. Occasionally mix the sangria as you serve it.

DEE ROLDAN'S BEEF EMPANADAS

As the meat cooks, guests love to nibble on a little something as they sip beer, Argentine wine, or sangria. These meat-filled pastries make excellent snacks. The recipe, supplied by Nic's mother, is a family favorite.

Makes about 22 empanadas

3½	cups all-purpose flour
1	teaspoon salt
1	cup (2 sticks) salted butter, chilled and cut into small cubes
3	large eggs
2	tablespoons white wine vinegar
3	tablespoons extra-virgin olive oil
1	cup minced yellow onion
3	cloves garlic, minced
1	pound ground sirloin
2	tablespoons ground cumin
1	teaspoon chili powder
2	teaspoons sugar
½	cup golden raisins
4	large hard-boiled eggs, chopped
1	cup green olives, sliced (optional)
	Salt and freshly ground black pepper

Sift the flour and salt into a large bowl. Blend in the butter cubes with your fingers until the flour mixture has an even, coarse texture.

In a separate bowl, beat together 2 of the eggs, ⅔ cup water, and the vinegar. Stir into the flour mixture.

Place the empanada dough on a floured surface. Knead it with the heel of your hand to bring the dough together. Cover the dough and let it rest in a cool place for at least an hour (it's best when refrigerated overnight).

Roll the dough out into a ¹/₈-inch-thick layer. Cut the dough into 4-inch circles with a round cookie or biscuit cutter and lightly flour them.

To make the filling, in a large saucepan, heat the olive oil over medium heat. Add the onions and garlic and cook until the onions become translucent, 5 to 7 minutes. Add the ground sirloin, breaking it up with a spoon, and cook, stirring, until lightly browned, about 10 minutes. Drain off the fat. Add the cumin, chili powder, sugar, and raisins, then add the chopped hard-boiled eggs and olives, if using, and carefully stir them into the meat mixture. Season with salt and pepper. Set aside.

Preheat the oven to 400°F and grease a cookie sheet.

To stuff the empanada-dough wrappers, place 1 tablespoon of filling in the center of each wrapper and dampen the outer perimeter of the dough with water. Carefully fold over the circle with the contents, forming a semicircle. Crimp down the edges with a fork all along the length of the folded side.

Place the folded empanadas on the prepared cookie sheet. Beat the remaining egg in a small bowl and brush the tops of the empanadas (this will give the empanadas a nice golden brown color). Bake for 15 to 20 minutes, or until golden brown. Serve hot.

MIXED GRILL ASADO

From the cities to the estancias to the pampas, the asado *is widely loved by Argentines. This traditional barbecue is all about the meat, so plan on a pound per person. Since the quality of the meat is key, Nic sources his cuts from noncommercial butchers familiar with the Argentine style of grilling.*

Every ranchero *has his favorite cuts. These are Nic's choices:*

Costillas	Beef ribs
Entraña	Skirt steak
Lomo	Filet, tenderloin
Morcilla	Blood sausage
Chorizo	Spicy sausage
Chinchulines	Small intestines
Mollejas	Sweetbreads

To prep the meat, Nic favors a simple rub with coarse sea salt, which brings out the flavor of the meat without adding superficial tastes.

For a traditional Argentinean barbecue, an *asador*, or grill master, digs a pit in the earth and fills it with coals and firewood. He lights the pile and lets it burn until it glows red, then spreads out the embers to create the *brasa*, or fire base. The grill, a portable steel or iron frame structure with four posts, is placed about eight inches above the *brasa*. The meat cooks for about thirty minutes, but that varies depending on desired doneness.

All of the above cuts can be grilled conventionally on a gas or charcoal grill.

To serve, the meat can be accompanied by a *chimichurri*, a savory sauce made with extra-virgin olive oil, red wine vinegar, red pepper flakes, garlic, and herbs. But most often, Nic serves it au naturel, with fresh country bread. "If you have great meat," he says, "everything else is incidental."

RAUL ROLDAN'S MATÉ

Drinking maté (yerba tea) in Argentina became popular in the mid-seventeenth century, when Spanish settlers arrived in the north of the country. The gauchos were the first to discover maté, but the tea has since garnered wider appeal. The maté is traditionally enjoyed in social settings and gatherings with friends and family. The same gourd and bombilla (metal strainer straw) is passed to everyone at the gathering. Nic's father, Raul, is seldom seen without a maté gourd in hand. This is his recipe.

Serves 1

Yerba maté loose tea

Spoon tea into the maté gourd until it is two thirds full. Place the bombilla into the gourd. Don't move the bombilla after it's in the maté.

Pour in cold water, filling to just below the top of the tea. Allow the maté to absorb the water.

Warm water to about 150°F. (The water should never boil; it is best to keep warm water in a thermos.) Pour warm water into the maté, filling the gourd to just below the top. Sip through the bombilla.

Note: Sugar may be added if desired (Argentine gauchos drink bitter maté).

Mixed Green Salad with
Green Apples and Walnuts

AN OFFERING OF LOVE
CONNIE BEAUDOIN AND SARA GROFF

IN YOGA, ONE OF THE MOST FUNDAMENTAL teachings is that of *ahimsa*. It upholds the path of nonviolence, of doing no harm to any living thing.

For yogini Connie Beaudoin, *ahimsa* is not limited to her practice within the yoga studio. It extends to every aspect of life—including entertaining. "For me," says Connie, who owns the popular Parasutra studio on the island, "a gathering is an act of love. It is a way for us to make space for each other."

On this late-spring night, Connie is cohosting, with student Sara Groff, a group of friends at the Palm Beach home of Merrilyn Bardes, mother of Sara's fiancé, Piper Quinn. The Palm Beach yoga community, which includes everyone from working moms to billionaires, gathers often, sometimes for simple potlucks at each other's homes, and other times to introduce an interesting new person or lifestyle option. Everyone takes turns bringing something to the table.

Sara sees it as yet another expression of yoga, which is, for her, a total lifestyle. "The underlying theme of all our gatherings is to engage in things that are authentic and meaningful," she says. "We focus on connecting with people. It's not about formality; it's about gratitude."

Tonight's festivities are held outdoors—the closer to nature, the better—on a terrace that overlooks the pool, lawn, and a magnificent specimen of banyan tree. The first thing guests encounter is an altar. It serves as a reminder of human bonds, as it is decorated with framed photos of Rwandan women who Connie has taught and befriended on past outreach trips.

Dinner is served on a low table, around which are arranged floor cushions strewn with blossoms of pink bougainvillea. Napkins are held with *mala* beads from Connie's collection, and place cards are inscribed with a mantra: "Earth, water, fire, air, and space have come together to make this meal. May we be nourished so that we may nourish life."

To Connie and Sara, nourishment is best derived from living foods. A raw, vegan diet is another way to practice *ahimsa*. "A plant-based diet, from my personal perspective and from the teachings of yoga, is a path of least harm—to ourselves, to the planet, and to our fellow creatures," says Connie.

Today's menu, prepared by raw chef and fellow yoga devotee Christopher Slawson, includes creative uncooked fare, such as taco "meat" made of walnuts, sun-dried tomatoes, and spices; "cheeses" made with various tree nuts; and savory crackers made with sprouted grains and herbs.

A relaxing tea of organic lemon balm, rose petals, valerian root, lemon myrtle, and chamomile is served poolside in pottery bowls made by yoga instructor Sara Lerner. Lerner's hand-sculpted, organic pots are etched with Sanskrit words that reinforce the concept of living consciously. "Things that are of the earth, that we can continue to use, are always preferable," says Connie of the vessels. "And these are so inspiring, which is another reason to use them."

The guests, resplendent in breezy whites, meander across the grounds, enjoying the warm breezes as they sip tea and nibble on almond butter balls and moca maca chip ice cream. Food is central to this get-together, but the real nourishment here is love.

Earth, Water, Fire, Air and Space.
Have come together to make this meal.
May we be nourished, so
that we may nourish life.

ॐ
CONNIE

MINI TOSTADAS

Some of the ingredients may be prepared in advance for easier assembly on the day of serving. The taco "meat" may be made in large batches and frozen. Though it seems daunting, this dish is truly delicious and worth the effort.

Makes 8 to 10 mini tostadas (served as an hors d'oeuvre)

> Herbed Flax Crackers, store-bought
> Macadamia Nut Ricotta (recipe follows)
> Walnut Taco Meat (recipe follows)
> Jalapeño Coleslaw (recipe follows)
> Pico de Gallo (recipe follows)
> Thin jalapeño slices for garnish

Place the herbed flax crackers on a decorative plate and spread macadamia ricotta over the tops.

Add a layer of walnut taco meat and jalapeño coleslaw. Finish with pico de gallo and garnish with thin slices of jalapeño.

MACADAMIA NUT RICOTTA

We love the addition of spinach to this recipe for its powerful punch of vitamin K and calcium. Leave out the spinach to achieve a true ricotta look and greater macadamia flavor.

Makes 2 cups

2	cups macadamia nuts, soaked in purified water at room temperature for 1 to 2 hours, drained and rinsed
1	tablespoon chopped fresh basil
1	tablespoon chopped fresh oregano
1	tablespoon onion powder
1	cup shredded spinach
½	teaspoon pink Himalayan salt
1	tablespoon fresh lemon juice

Place all the ingredients in a high-speed blender, add ½ cup filtered water, and blend until smooth. If needed, add more water to reach the desired consistency (it should be smooth like ricotta). The ricotta can easily be made ahead of time and stored in the refrigerator for up to 3 days.

WALNUT TACO "MEAT"

Makes 3 cups

- 4 cups walnuts, soaked in purified water at room temperature for 6 hours, drained and rinsed
- 2 teaspoons ground cumin
  Pinch of jalapeño powder
- ½ cup coconut nectar
- ½ cup chopped sun-dried tomatoes
  Pinch of pink Himalayan salt

Place the walnuts on a dehydrator tray and dehydrate at 105°F for 24 to 36 hours, or until they are dry all the way through.

Place the walnuts in a food processor and process until broken down, being careful not to overprocess into a paste. Transfer to a large bowl, add the remaining ingredients, and mix well.

JALAPEÑO COLESLAW

Makes 8 cups

- 1 small head green cabbage
- 1 cup chopped Pickled Jalapeños, store-bought
- 1 small carrot, cut into juilienne
- ½ cup cilantro leaves
- ¼ cup cherry tomatoes, halved
  Cumin Dressing (recipe follows)

Using a mandoline food slicer on the thinnest setting, carefully shred the cabbage onto a clean work surface.

In a large bowl, combine the cabbage, pickled jalapeños, carrots, cilantro, and cherry tomatoes. Toss with the cumin dressing.

CUMIN DRESSING

Makes ¹⁄₂ cup

- 3 tablespoons fresh orange juice
- 2 tablespoons fresh lemon juice
- ½ teaspoon coconut palm sugar
- ½ teaspoon ground cumin
- ¼ teaspoon Pink Himalayan salt
- ¼ teaspoon freshly ground black pepper
- ⅓ cup cold-pressed olive oil

In a small bowl, whisk together all the ingredients except the olive oil. Add the oil in a slow, steady stream, whisking constantly until smooth. Use immediately, or cover and refrigerate for up to 3 days. Whisk before serving.

PICO DE GALLO

Makes 3 cups

- 2 cups chopped, seeded tomatoes
- ½ cup chopped white onion
- 1 cup fresh cilantro leaves, chopped
- ¼ cup fresh lime juice
- 1 jalapeño, seeded and finely chopped
  Pink Himalayan salt to taste

Place all the ingredients in a large mixing bowl and toss. The pico de gallo can be refrigerated for up to 3 days.

SPRING GARDEN SALAD WITH WILDFLOWER HONEY-MUSTARD DRESSING AND CANDIED WALNUTS

This fresh, wholesome salad is a delicous way to enjoy the benefits of living foods.

Serves 4

- 1 cucumber, peeled and thinly sliced
- ¾ cup baby arugula leaves
- ½ cup Bibb lettuce leaves
- 1 cup sunflower sprouts
- 1 tablespoon hemp seeds
  Wildflower Honey-Mustard Dressing (recipe follows)
- 1 cup mixed seasonal berries
- ¼ cup Candied Walnuts (page 95)

Top: Spring Garden Salad;
Bottom left: Spicy Asian Lettuce Cups;
Bottom right: Mini Tostadas

Top: Almond Cracker and Tree Nut Cheeses in Superfood Salad; Bottom: Baby Dragon Bowl with Five-Spice Dressing

Create a cucumber wrapper by cutting the ends off of the cucumber, peeling it, then slicing it in half crosswise. Holding a cucumber half against an 8-inch knife, carefully make a thin spiraling cut around the outside of the cucumber, creating a nori-like sheet. Toss any lingering seeds and slice off uneven edges.

Combine the arugula, Bibb lettuce, sunflower sprouts, and hemp seeds in a large bowl. Toss with the dressing.

Place the cucumber wrappers on a small serving plate and fill with the salad mixture. Garnish with the berries and candied walnuts.

WILDFLOWER HONEY-MUSTARD DRESSING

Makes 2 ½ cups

1	cup coconut vinegar
¼	cup raw wildflower honey
1	cup cold-pressed olive oil
¼	cup ground mustard

Place all the ingredients in a high-speed blender and blend until smooth.

CANDIED WALNUTS

A delicious addition of omega-3s, adding flavor and crunch to any salad, these candied walnuts are a tasty snack on their own and we love to chop them up and toss over oatmeal.

Makes 1 cup

1	cup walnuts
½	cup coconut palm sugar
½	cup maple syrup

Soak the walnuts in purified water at room temperature for 6 to 8 hours, rinsing every 2 hours. Drain and place the walnuts in a large bowl; add the palm sugar and maple syrup and stir to coat thoroughly.

Place the coated walnuts in a single layer on Teflex or ParaFlexx sheets on dehydrator trays and dehydrate at 115°F for 24 to 36 hours. Cool to room temperature before serving.

SUPERFOOD SALAD WITH SPIRULINA DRESSING

Rich in many vitamins and calcium, kale is a wonder vegetable. When combined with spirulina, said to be a nutritionally complete food, the health benefits are stellar.

Serves 4

½	cup arame seaweed
2	cups shredded green kale
1	cup arugula leaves
	Spirulina Dressing (recipe follows)
½	avocado, peeled, pitted, and thinly sliced
1	small beet, julienned or grated
1	cup sunflower sprouts

Soak the arame in water for 5 to 10 minutes until soft. Carefully drain the delicate sheets and set aside.

Combine the kale and arugula in a large bowl and toss with the dressing. Transfer to a serving bowl, add the avocado, beet, and sunflower sprouts, and top with the arame.

SPIRULINA DRESSING

Makes 1 cup

½	cup coconut vinegar
2	tablespoons raw honey
½	cup cold-pressed olive oil
¼	cup prepared mustard
1½	teaspoons spirulina powder

Combine all the ingredients in a blender and blend until smooth. Any unused dressing can be stored in the refrigerator for up to 5 days.

BABY DRAGON BOWL WITH FIVE-SPICE DRESSING

The julienned zucchini has a noodlelike texture, and the dressing has an exotic flavor that recalls North African cuisine. Truly unique and delicious.

Serves 4

3	cups julienned zucchini
½	cup chopped red bell pepper
½	cup chopped broccoli
½	cup chopped baby bok choy
¼	cup fresh cilantro leaves
	Five-Spice Dressing (recipe follows)
½	cup almonds, coarsely chopped, store-bought
¼	cup fresh lemon juice
¼	cup cold-pressed olive oil
	Pinch of pink Himalayan salt

In a large bowl, combine the zucchini, bell pepper, broccoli, boy choy, and cilantro.

Toss with dressing and top with the chopped almonds.

FIVE-SPICE DRESSING

Makes 1 cup

¼	cup wheat-free tamari
1	tablespoon coconut vinegar
¼	teaspoon five-spice powder
3	tablespoons sesame oil
1	to 2 tablespoons raw almond butter
2	teaspoons peeled and finely minced fresh ginger

Whisk all the ingredients together in a small bowl. Any unused dressing can be stored in the refrigerator up to 4 days.

ALMOND BUTTER BALLS

This is one sweet treat that is actually good for you. Keep plenty on hand to serve with tea any time of day.

Makes approximately 50 balls

4	cups organic Italian almond flour or almond meal
1	cup raw almond butter
1	cup maple syrup
2	tablespoons cold-pressed olive oil
	Pinch of pink Himalayan salt
½	cup hemp seeds
¾	cup coconut palm sugar

Place all the ingredients in a food processor, reserving 2 tablespoons of hemp seeds and 2 tablespoons of palm sugar for the topping, and process until smooth. Using a small melon baller, scoop out the mixture, forming it into bite-size balls.

Combine the reserved hemp seeds and palm sugar in a shallow bowl. Roll the balls in the mixture to coat. Other healthful toppings to try: raw coconut, raw cacao nibs, or crushed nuts.

MOCHA MACA CHIP ICE CREAM

Though there is no actual cream (or dairy of any kind) in this dessert, you won't believe how much it tastes like traditional ice cream.

Makes 2 quarts

2	cups raw cashews, soaked for 4 hours in purified water at room temperature, drained and rinsed
2	cups organic French-pressed coffee
1	cup unrefined coconut oil
½	cup raw honey
1	vanilla bean, scraped
2	tablespoons organic raw maca powder
¼	cup raw cacao nibs

Combine all the ingredients except the cacao nibs in a blender and blend until very smooth. Pour the mixture into an ice-cream maker and churn according to the manufacturer's instructions. When the mixture is the consistency of soft-serve ice cream, add the cacao nibs.

Transfer to an airtight container and freeze until completely firm, about 3 hours. Remove from the freezer 10 minutes before serving.

Top left (clockwise from top): Brownie Sundae with Bananas; Mint Chip Bark; Mocha Maca Chip Ice Cream with Macaroons; Citrus Cookies, Handmade Chocolates, and Almond Butter Balls; Pumpkin-Seed Buttercups

FORMALLY SPEAKING
ENTERTAINING IN
THE GILDED AGE TRADITION

A ROYAL EVENING
HILARY AND WILBUR ROSS

HAVING GROWN UP IN NEW YORK CITY and Southampton, Hilary Geary Ross was exposed at a very early age to dazzling parties. "In the 1960s," she recalls, "I was visiting my cousins Heidi and Alfred Vanderbilt at my aunt Jeanne Vanderbilt's beautiful East Side town house the night she gave a dinner attended by Liz Taylor, Joe Mankiewicz, Montgomery Clift, and other Hollywood legends. I also remember the fabulous coming-out party with a *Gone with the Wind* theme in honor of my pal Scarlett Leas, hosted by her mother, Fernanda Wanamaker Leas, in Southampton. Everyone was in costume, and horse-drawn buggies brought you up the long driveway to the house."

With such a frame of reference, it is little wonder Hilary is now known as one of the most glamorous hostesses in Palm Beach and New York. She and husband Wilbur, chairman and CEO of WL Ross & Co. LLC, adore entertaining and have feted everyone from celebrated photographer Harry Benson to Silas Chou, Wilbur's Chinese business partner.

Windsong, their John L. Volk–designed Georgian Revival mansion along "the lake"— the Intracoastal Waterway—lends itself equally to grand affairs and intimate gatherings. "It's a wonderful house for big parties and a wonderful house for small parties," Hilary says of the 10,000-square-foot manse with interiors by New York designer Bunny Williams. "There is space, but it's not unwieldy."

While the Rosses may be known in certain circles for their lavish hospitality (and for amassing one of the world's foremost collections of contemporary art), the hostess's focus remains steadfastly on her guests. "To surprise the seasoned partygoer who has seen it all, I try to introduce him or her to someone new, who hopefully will become a friend," she says. "Friendship, to me, is the ultimate gift."

Tonight the Rosses are celebrating their friendship with the Duke and Duchess of Marlborough by hosting a party in their honor. "I like to do a dinner in someone's honor, as it adds a touch of festivity to the party," Hilary says.

At this festive dinner, hosted in the ballroom of the Rosses' guest house, the who's who of New York, Palm Beach, and beyond flows through Windsong as cocktails, crab cakes, and crudités are passed. They find their place at the table by glancing at the embossed leather seating charts, designed by Hilary and fabricated by an East Hampton bookbinder.

As the sun sets over the Intracoastal, guests stroll through the immaculate formal gardens, studded with prized sculptures and candlelit lanterns, and make their way to the ballroom for dinner. The modern acrylic dining table, set upon frosted pedestals, is complemented by ghost chairs and set with a traditional arrangement of fresh moss and hundreds of spring tulips from end to end.

The menu has been selected with the guests' well-being in mind. Hilary believes that a healthy menu—excepting a delectable dessert, of course—helps guests enjoy a meal with friends without fretting over the high caloric intake that often goes hand in hand with a bustling social season.

As guests converse across the long table and courses are served on gorgeous china by Anna Weatherley, Herend, and Mottahedeh, the evening takes on a dynamic dimension. Another success in a long-standing tradition of hosting extraordinary parties.

"Giving parties can be highly creative, even artistic," Hilary says, "and certainly great fun."

ASPARAGUS CHARLOTTE WITH BELUGA CAVIAR

HEIRLOOM TOMATO SALAD

PISTACHIO-CRUSTED CHILEAN SEA BASS

GRILLED LOBSTER WITH PISTACHIO LEMON BUTTER

GRILLED SALMON
WITH ASPARAGUS AND TOMATO COULIS

SPRING VEGETABLES WITH HERB VINAIGRETTE

COCONUT AND MACADAMIA ICE CREAM BALLS
WITH RASPBERRY SAUCE

HEIRLOOM TOMATO SALAD

Your local farmers' market is the place to find fabulous heirloom tomatoes. We are fortunate to have the West Palm Beach market so near, where Walter Ross's (no relation!) tomatoes can be found every weekend during the season.

Serves 4

1½	pounds large heirloom tomatoes, sliced into wedges
2	teaspoons white balsamic vinegar
2	teaspoons Dijon-style mustard
2	teaspoons minced garlic
2	teaspoons finely chopped fresh oregano
2	tablespoons extra-virgin olive oil
	Salt and freshly ground black pepper
2	tablespoons chopped fresh flat-leaf parsley

Arrange the tomato wedges in a decorative bowl.

In a small bowl, whisk together the vinegar, mustard, garlic, oregano, and olive oil. Season with salt and pepper. Pour over the tomatoes and set aside. Toss the tomatoes with the parsley just before serving.

PISTACHIO-CRUSTED CHILEAN SEA BASS

This is a perfect choice for entertaining, as the fish is cooked in the oven, not on the stove top, thus avoiding any unpleasant odors.

Serves 4

1½	cups shelled pistachios
3	cups multigrain flakes or whole-wheat bread crumbs
4	(6- to 7-ounce) Chilean sea bass fillets
⅔	cup Dijon-style mustard

Preheat the oven to 350°F.

In a food processor, pulse the pistachios and multigrain flakes until fine. Transfer to a shallow bowl.

Coat each piece of bass with mustard on both sides. Dredge the mustard-coated fish in the cereal mixture and place on a baking sheet.

Place in the oven and bake for about 25 minutes, or until the fish is opaque and cooked through. Serve immediately.

Pistachio-Crusted
Chilean Sea Bass over
Spring Vegetables with
Herb Vinaigrette

GRILLED LOBSTER WITH PISTACHIO LEMON BUTTER

Serves 4

½	cup raw, unsalted, shelled pistachios
4	tablespoons (½ stick) unsalted butter, at room temperature
	Rind of 1 preserved lemon
1	tablespoon chopped fresh flat-leaf parsley
	Sea salt and freshly ground black pepper
4	(¼-pound) lobster tails
1	lemon, sliced, for garnish

Preheat the broiler.

In a food processor, combine the pistachios, butter, lemon rind, and parsley. Season with salt and pepper and pulse until just combined.

Spread the lemon butter mixture over the lobster flesh and place on a baking sheet. Place under the broiler and broil for 8 minutes, or until the lobster is cooked through. To serve, arrange the lobster tails on a platter and garnish with the lemon slices.

GRILLED SALMON WITH ASPARAGUS AND TOMATO COULIS

Serves 4

8	tablespoons extra-virgin olive oil
3	pounds green or white asparagus, ends trimmed
3	cloves garlic, chopped
¼	cup chicken broth, preferably low-sodium
1	teaspoon soy sauce, preferably low-sodium
⅔	cup finely chopped fresh chives
½	medium yellow onion, chopped
2	large tomatoes, chopped
	Salt and freshly ground black pepper
2	tablespoons sugar
4	(6-ounce) center-cut salmon fillets
12	basil leaves, julienned

Preheat the oven to 325°F.

In a large sauté pan, heat 5 tablespoons of the olive oil over medium heat. Add the asparagus and garlic and cook until the asparagus begins to caramelize, about 6 minutes. Add the broth, bring to a simmer, and simmer until it is almost completely absorbed, about 8 minutes. Add the soy sauce and cook until it is absorbed, about 1 minute. Remove from the heat, transfer to a plate, and set aside to cool. Add the chives.

Wipe out the pan and heat 2 tablespoons of the remaining olive oil over medium heat. Add the onions and sauté until translucent. Add the tomatoes, season with salt and pepper, and add the sugar. Cook until the tomatoes are very tender, about 12 minutes. Remove from the heat, and when cool enough to handle, transfer the tomatoes to a blender and puree until very fine. Strain through a fine-mesh sieve and set aside. This is the tomato coulis.

Place the salmon fillets on a baking sheet. Cut three quarters of the way through the middle of each piece and arrange a few asparagus pieces in the slit. Season the salmon with salt and pepper and drizzle with the remaining 1 tablespoon of olive oil.

Place in the oven and bake for about 15 minutes, or until the salmon is cooked to your liking.

To serve, spread the tomato coulis on the bottom of a serving platter, arrange the salmon pieces on top, and garnish with the basil.

Asparagus Charlotte
with Beluga Caviar

SPRING VEGETABLES WITH HERB VINAIGRETTE

Serves 4

1	bunch fresh chervil
1	bunch fresh basil
3	tablespoons Kalamata olive oil
1	teaspoon balsamic vinegar
2	tablespoons sherry vinegar
	Juice of 1 lime
4	young carrots (with leaves)
4	mini zucchini
4	baby eggplants
	Basil leaves or edible borage flowers for garnish

Place the chervil, basil, olive oil, balsamic vinegar, sherry vinegar, and lime juice in the bowl of a food processor and process until all the herbs are finely chopped. Peel the carrots, leaving some of the green leaves, and cut the zucchini lengthwise into ¼-inch slices. Cut the eggplants in half lengthwise.

Steam all the vegetables, making sure they remain al dente (baby carrots will take 8 to 10 minutes; baby zucchini will take 6 to 8 minutes; baby eggplant will take about 10 minutes). (Optional: Grill the eggplant for 2 minutes for added flavor and texture.)

Arrange the steamed vegetables on a decorative plate, drizzle with the vinaigrette, and garnish with basil leaves or borage flowers. Serve immediately.

COCONUT AND MACADAMIA ICE-CREAM BALLS WITH RASPBERRY SAUCE

The combination of flavors in this dessert is elegant and delightful. On another occasion try vanilla, chocolate, or caramel ice cream. It is also fabulous to combine flavors, serving a few balls of coconut ice cream with one vanilla ball to surprise the palate.

Serves 4

3	cups unsweetened shredded coconut
2	cups roasted macadamia nuts
2	pints coconut ice cream
2	cups raspberries
½	cup sugar
	Juice of 1 lime

Preheat the oven to 350°F and line a baking sheet with parchment paper.

Place the coconut and macadamia nuts on the prepared baking sheet, place in the oven, and toast until lightly golden, 5 to 7 minutes. Transfer to a plate to cool.

Using an ice-cream scoop or large melon baller, make 8 balls with the ice cream. Coat with the coconut-macadamia mixture and return to the freezer until ready to serve.

In a blender, puree the raspberries, sugar, and lime juice until smooth. Refrigerate until ready to serve.

Serve the ice cream balls in a decorative glass bowl, passing the raspberry sauce on the side.

NANCY G. BRINKER

Seafood Cocktail
served with Soda Bread

Organic Chicken Breast
served with Lemon Zest Caper Sauce

Mushroom Risotto

English Peas, Baby Carrots,
Roasted Spring Onions

Assorted Dessert Tarts
Chocolate, Lemon, Strawberry Shortcake

STATE OF THE PARTY
AMBASSADOR NANCY BRINKER

DURING HER ILLUSTRIOUS CAREER AS chief of protocol for the George W. Bush White House, U.S. ambassador to Hungary, and CEO and founder of Susan G. Komen Race for the Cure, Nancy Brinker has had the opportunity to meet and entertain interesting people from every segment of society—world leaders, scholars, philanthropists, business leaders, and volunteers. She has learned something from each of them.

Take the art of gift giving, for example. "Laura Bush is one of the great gift givers," Ambassador Brinker says. "Gifts can be simple, humorous, or functional; things that people don't often have time to buy for themselves."

She also has taken entertaining cues from hostess Marjorie Fisher, from whom she discovered, "When you invite someone to your home, you are saying, 'You are important to me.' A great hostess asks, 'How do I express that?'" By creating a welcoming atmosphere and an enjoyable experience that shows you care about how they feel, she notes. "The food must be tasty and the guests interesting. The table should be pretty but not overwhelming. It should all feel comfortable. Don't worry about overdecorating."

For this intimate gathering, Ambassador Brinker has stayed true to her philosophy. Upon entering her home, guests are surrounded by her collection of Hungarian art, beautiful books, and an atmosphere of warmth and genuine welcome. Guests are greeted with wine glasses that bear the presidential seal, a nod to her service as chief of protocol.

Dinner is served on her collection of Anna Weatherley china, chosen not only for its beauty but also for its heritage. "Anna is Hungarian and comes from a great tradition of those who created hand-painted porcelain," she says. During her service as U.S. ambassador to Hungary, she "wanted to take something to Hungary—a table service—to entertain Hungarians by celebrating their great sculptors, talented designers, and master painters."

Always serve drinks to guests as they enter your home. Be sure to have both alcoholic and nonalcoholic beverages available.

Choose music carefully, as it provides nice entertainment and ambiance for the evening.

Putting guests at ease is simply personal engagement. Chat with friends in a warm, friendly way about things that interest them: their family, home, education, and goals.

Don't put too much on the table. When it comes to flowers, restraint is better than overflowering. Don't overwhelm your guests.

Seat guests near others they will enjoy.

Spouses do not always have to be separated from each other.

Be sure the food is tasty, your guests are interesting, and the table is pretty.

She says one of her passions is to "create connectivity between people and causes," and that often happens in a social setting. She has had great role models in that regard, beginning with her own family. She recalls the fabulous dinners hosted by her aunt and uncle in their lovely home, and not only because they were so beautifully executed. "Warmth, great food, and great conversation" is what she remembers most vividly, and now infuses those elements into her own parties.

Ambassador Brinker has a remarkable ability to gather the most fascinating people and spark passionate discussions that include everyone. So guests linger, even when they have a pressing engagement. "When people leave a party, what they remember most is how they feel," she says. "Mother always said it is all about others, not about you. Be thoughtful, and make sure your guests have what they need and feel good about where they are."

SEAFOOD COCKTAIL

Brandy gives this sauce its unexpected flavor and sensational aroma.

Serves 4

2	cups small, halved cherry tomatoes, reserve a few for garnish
2	cups peeled and diced seedless cucumber
8	ounces lump crabmeat, picked over and cleaned
24	medium shrimp, cooked and peeled, reserve 4 for garnish
¼	cup mayonnaise
¼	cup ketchup
4	teaspoons horseradish
4	drops Tabasco sauce
¼	cup brandy
¾	cup heavy cream

In a transparent cup or bowl, layer ¼ of the tomatoes, then ¼ of the cucumber, crabmeat, and 5 of the shrimp. Repeat this procedure three more times.

In a medium bowl, whisk together the mayonnaise, ketchup, horseradish, Tabasco, brandy, and heavy cream until smooth. Pour the mixture over the seafood to cover the top. Garnish with the remaining 4 shrimp and cherry tomatoes.

SODA BREAD

If you are lucky enough to have any soda bread left over, it is delicious for breakfast with black tea or coffee.

Makes 1 loaf

1	tablespoon unsalted butter for greasing the pan
2	cups all-purpose flour
1	tablespoon sugar
2	tablespoons baking powder
½	teaspoon baking soda
½	teaspoon salt
4	tablespoons (½ stick) unsalted butter, melted
1	cup currants
1	large egg, beaten
1	cup buttermilk

Preheat the oven to 375°F and butter a baking dish.

In a large bowl, mix together the flour, sugar, baking powder, baking soda, and salt. In a small bowl, mix together the melted butter, currants, egg, and buttermilk. Add to the flour mixture and mix until just combined. Do not overmix.

Form the dough into a flat circle or a loaflike shape. Place on the buttered dish, place in the oven, and bake for about 40 minutes, or until the top is golden. Cool completely in the baking dish before serving, then transfer to a serving platter. To serve, cut into 1-inch slices.

Top left: Seafood Cocktail; Bottom: Organic Chicken Breast with Lemon-Caper Sauce and Frisée Salad

ORGANIC CHICKEN BREAST WITH LEMON-CAPER SAUCE AND FRISÉE SALAD

Serves 4

4	(6-ounce) organic boneless, skinless chicken breasts
	Salt and freshly ground black pepper
1	cup fresh lemon juice
1	cup dry white wine
1	cup (2 sticks) unsalted butter
2	tablespoons capers, rinsed
	Peel from 1 large lemon (yellow part only)
6	ounces frisée salad leaves

Preheat the oven to 350°F.

Season the chicken breasts with salt and pepper, place in a baking dish, and cook in the oven for 15 to 20 minutes, or until cooked through.

In a saucepan, combine the lemon juice, wine, butter, and capers and heat, whisking, until the butter is melted and the capers begin to crisp, about 5 minutes.

Bring a small saucepan of water to a boil; add the lemon rind and boil until very soft, about 10 minutes. Drain and cut into slivers to use as a garnish.

To serve, arrange the frisée leaves among 4 plates, top each with a chicken breast, spoon over the lemon-caper sauce, and garnish with the slivers of lemon peel.

MUSHROOM RISOTTO

You can include any of your favorites mushrooms in this risotto, such as chanterelle, baby portobello, white, and shiitake.

Serves 4

3	cups chicken broth, preferably homemade or low-sodium organic
4	tablespoons (½ stick) unsalted butter
2	tablespoons extra-virgin olive oil
½	cup diced yellow onion
1½	cups sliced assorted mushrooms
½	cup Arborio rice
1	cup dry white wine
	Salt and freshly ground black pepper
¼	cup grated Parmesan cheese, plus more to pass at the table

Bring the broth to a simmer in a medium saucepan over medium-low heat. Keep the broth warm at a low heat.

In a large saucepan, heat the butter and olive oil over medium heat until the butter is melted. Add the onions and mushrooms and sauté until the onions are translucent and the mushrooms release all their juices, 10 to 12 minutes. Add the rice and stir to coat with the butter and oil. Cook for about one minute.

Add the warm broth, ½ cup at a time, stirring between each addition until the rice has absorbed most of the liquid. After the final ½ cup of broth has been added and absorbed, add the wine and keep stirring until it is all absorbed by the rice. Season with salt and pepper and stir in the cheese just before serving. Pass additional cheese at the table.

CHOCOLATE TARTS

Serves 4

4	tablespoons (½ stick) unsalted butter, at room temperature, plus more for greasing
¼	cup powdered sugar
	Pinch of salt
1	large egg yolk
½	cup all-purpose flour
¼	cup unsweetened Dutch-processed cocoa powder
¼	cup chopped bittersweet chocolate, melted
1	teaspoon brandy
¼	cup heavy cream
4	whole strawberries for garnish

In a large bowl, beat the butter, powdered sugar, and salt together until pale in color. Add the egg and mix well. Add the flour and cocoa powder and form the mixture into a ball. Wrap in plastic and refrigerate for at least 1 hour and up to 3 hours.

Preheat the oven to 350°F.

Roll the dough to a ¼-inch thickness and cut out 4 circles to line 4 holes of a muffin pan. Butter the pan and line with the chocolate dough. Place in the oven and bake for about 8 minutes, until the shell is cooked. Remove from the oven and cool in the pan until cool enough to transfer to a decorative serving platter or individual plates.

In a small bowl, mix the chocolate and brandy together. In a medium bowl, whip the heavy cream until fluffy. Add the chocolate and brandy mixture and mix well. Divide the mixture among the chocolate shells and refrigerate until ready to serve.

rtars Magyar Művészet

mporary Hungarian Art Zeitgenössische ungarische Kunst

Körmendi-Cs.
Gyűjtemény Collection Sam

A MUSICAL EVENING
PATRICK PARK

EVEN BEFORE ENTERING Patrick Park's palatial home in Jupiter, guests know they are in for a good time. At the motor court by the front entrance, a trio of mariachis plays lively Mexican tunes, welcoming friends and setting the stage for a night bristling with memories in the making.

For Patrick, music is an integral part of entertaining. A classically trained pianist with a passion for music of all kinds, he incorporates musical elements into every one of his parties. "When it comes to hospitality," he says, "music is, for me, at the top of the list. I always hope the food is good, but I make sure the music is."

He even designed his home with music in mind. The dining area is not a dedicated room but rather an open space between the living room and the bar. This presents opportunities for live music during dinner and allows guests to move around—even dance—between courses.

For this dinner party with friends, Patrick has brought in well-loved Palm Beach/ Boston pianist David Crohan, who has been playing on the island since 1990. Crohan plays Patrick's Steinway, one of three grand pianos in the house, at the foot of the staircase as guests mingle at the bar, noshing on classic Palm Beach hors d'oeuvres like cheese puffs, caviar-topped smoked salmon, and beggar's purses.

As guests adjourn to the dining room for dinner, a Latin guitarist strums softly, accompanying all four courses, including a lobster salad served on a blue-neon-uplit slab of ice that elicits a collective "wow."

Dessert is rarely served at the table. "If the weather is good, we will have after-dinner drinks and dessert outside," Patrick says. "Other times, we might go upstairs. When I have guests, the house is one hundred percent open."

Tonight, finger desserts, including everyone's favorite chocolate-dipped cheesecake lollipops, and cordials are taken in the living room, where the evening's featured performance is staged. Guests are rapt as tenor Francesco Valpa belts out operatic arias, his voice filling every corner of the high-ceilinged room.

Patrick claps the loudest as Valpa takes a bow at the end of the evening. "What a voice," he beams. "It's important to me to have musicians who have talent and a passion."

Though he is as talented as the musicians he hires, he very rarely gets behind the piano himself. Since he never played professionally (he went into the family steel business

Music is the most important element of the evening and sets the tone for everything else.

The moment your friends drive up to the house, the party starts. I love to have them greeted by a lively mariachi band or trumpeters to announce their arrival. Guests walk in with a smile and are excited for what comes next.

Piano is perfect for cocktail hour. You can really enjoy both the music and the conversation.

Soft Latin guitar is another good choice for cocktail hour, and guests enjoy it during dinner, too. The music is beautiful but soft enough to have conversations with friends.

End the evening on a high note! Taking dessert in the living room lets guests really enjoy the featured performance of the evening.

The mariachi band is waiting for guests as they drive away, to leave them with one final memory of the evening. That is the icing on the cake.

instead), he considers himself "out of practice," so he leaves it to the professionals.

The same goes for the food. For his dinner parties, he personally chooses the menus, opting for universally loved comfort foods over complicated dishes. That's not to say that he doesn't sometimes cook himself. He enjoys barbecuing and calls himself "a great pancake chef."

For the latter, Patrick usually whips up his own batter. Sometimes, though, it's just not practical. For a breakfast he once hosted, he went to his favorite pancake restaurant—IHOP—and asked to buy a container of the famous batter (which, incidentally, is not for sale). By hook or by crook, they ended up selling it to him and he prepared it for his guests. On the menu card, he called it "Grandma's Pancakes."

"People were so impressed," he says with a laugh. "They really thought it tasted like Grandma's."

It just goes to show that presentation is everything. So it is with tonight's dinner party, where everything proceeds flawlessly, down to the exit of the guests. The mariachi band serenades Patrick's friends with high-energy strings and trumpets as they wait for the valets to deliver their cars.

"It's nice to leave people with a final memory," he says, "and to watch them leave with a smile."

PALM BEACH CHEESE PUFFS

No party is complete without this Palm Beach staple, and the variations are limitless. Of course, the classic cheese puff is a true pastry made with a pâte à choux dough, but this Palm Beach version is quick, easy, and delicious. Try diced scallions, peppers, or bits of bacon instead of the onion or you can spice them up with a dash of cayenne pepper. Add a burst of flavor with goat cheese in addition to the Parmesan.

Makes 20

- 2 cups mayonnaise
- 2 cups grated Parmesan cheese
- ½ cup finely chopped yellow onion
- 10 slices white bread

Preheat the oven to 350°F.

In a large bowl, mix together the mayonnaise, cheese, and onion.

Cut the bread into rounds using a 1-inch cutter (2 rounds per slice of bread) and arrange on a baking sheet. Place a heaping teaspoon of the mayonnaise-cheese spread on top, place in the oven, and bake for 6 to 8 minutes, until the tops turn golden. Transfer to a decorative plate and serve hot.

LOBSTER SALAD

This salad is simple to prepare, but the presentation makes all the difference. Park's neon-lit slab of ice is certainly spectacular, but a beautiful iced bowl or dish would be lovely as well. If you like a little spice, you can add a few dashes of Tabasco or Worcestershire sauce, a teaspoon of Dijon-style mustard, or a dash of Old Bay seasoning.

Serves 4

- 1 cup diced cooked lobster
- 1 tablespoon fresh lemon juice
- ½ cup thinly sliced celery
- ⅓ cup mayonnaise (just enough to hold the salad together)
- Salt and freshly ground black pepper
- 4 ounces mixed salad greens
- Garnishes (optional): avocado, bacon bits, chopped hard-boiled eggs

In a medium bowl, combine the lobster meat, lemon juice, celery, and mayonnaise. Season with salt and pepper and mix well.

To serve, divide the salad greens among 4 plates and top with the lobster salad. Finish with the garnishes of your choice.

Top left: Chicken Dim Sum;
Top right: Lobster Salad,
Bottom: Smoked Salmon in
Cucumber Cups

FOUR-CHEESE RAVIOLI

These tasty ravioli are lovely with your favorite tomato sauce, but they can also be tossed with lobster meat, butter, garlic, and spinach, and then topped with freshly grated Parmesan cheese for an elegant alternative. It makes a fabulous main course.

Serves 4

4	large eggs
1	teaspoon extra-virgin olive oil
1½	tablespoons water
2	cups all-purpose flour
	Pinch of salt
1	(8-ounce) container whole-milk ricotta cheese
1	(4-ounce) package cream cheese, softened
½	cup shredded mozzarella cheese
½	cup shredded provolone cheese
2	tablespoons finely chopped fresh flat-leaf parsley
1	(24-ounce) jar tomato sauce
	Chopped fresh basil for garnish

In a medium bowl, beat 2 of the eggs with the olive oil and water. Combine the flour and salt in a mound on your work surface and form a well at the center of the mound. Pour half the egg mixture into the well and gradually work the flour into the egg mixture. Add the remaining egg mixture and knead to form a smooth, elastic dough; this will take 8 to 10 minutes. Add more flour if the dough is too sticky or more water if it is too dry. Form the dough into a ball and wrap tightly with plastic. Refrigerate for 1 hour.

While the dough is resting, prepare the ravioli filling by combing the ricotta cheese, cream cheese, mozzarella cheese, provolone cheese, 1 of the remaining eggs, and the parsley in a large bowl. Mix well and set aside or cover and refrigerate until ready to use.

To form the ravioli, roll the pasta dough out into thin sheets, no thicker than a nickel. You can use a rolling pin, but a pasta machine works best. You may need to pass the dough through the machine a few times to get the desired thickness. The size of the sheets will vary according to the pasta machine used, but they should be at least 5 inches wide. It is important that your pasta sheet be thin enough so you can see your fingers through it, but not so thin that it's translucent.

In a small bowl, beat the remaining egg with 3 tablespoons of warm water for the egg wash.

To assemble the ravioli, brush the egg wash over a sheet of pasta. Drop the filling mixture on the pasta sheet by the teaspoonful, about a half inch from the edge and 1 inch apart from one another.

Carefully fold the pasta over so it covers the cheese filling, pressing out the air from around each portion of filling. Press firmly around the filling to seal. Cut into individual ravioli with a knife or pizza cutter and seal the edges with a fork.

Place a large pot of lightly salted water over high heat and bring to a rolling boil. Stir in the ravioli and return to a boil. Cook, stirring occasionally, until the ravioli float to the top and the filling is hot, 6 to 8 minutes. Drain well.

To serve, warm your favorite tomato sauce and spoon it over the ravioli. Garnish with fresh basil.

Fruit Sorbet; Opposite: Cheesecake
Pops, Nut Bars, and Chocolate-dipped
Strawberries

FRUIT SORBET

Two ingredients and a simple execution make this dessert a go-to for even the busiest host. Use your favorite fruits: blueberries, raspberries, strawberries, mango, and pear all work well. If fresh is not an option, frozen fruits are just as delicious.

Serves 4

- ¾ cup granulated sugar
- 2 cups fruit puree

Prepare a simple syrup by combining the sugar with ²/₃ cup of water in a medium saucepan. Place over medium-low heat and cook until the sugar is fully dissolved. Cool to room temperature, then transfer to a container, cover, and refrigerate until completely chilled, about an hour.

Combine the fruit and simple syrup in a blender and blend until smooth. Strain the mixture through a fine-mesh sieve to remove any seeds (use a spatula to aid in passing the puree through the strainer). Transfer to an ice-cream machine and churn according to the manufacturer's directions. Serve immediately or transfer to a container and allow to set in the freezer.

CHEESECAKE POPS

This fun, bite-size dessert is very versatile. You can vary the shape of the pops, the toppings, and the presentation. Instead of a lollipop stick, you can also try beautiful cocktail forks. Be sure to start this recipe at least a day in advance to allow ample freezing time.

Makes 24 pops

- 3 (8-ounce) packages cream cheese, at room temperature
- 1¹/₃ cups powdered sugar
- 5 large eggs
- ¼ cup all-purpose flour
- 2 tablespoons vanilla extract
- 2 tablespoons fresh lemon juice
- 3½ ounces dark chocolate, chopped
- 1 cup sprinkles, chopped nuts, or candied fruit for decoration

Preheat the oven to 325°F and grease a 9- or 10-inch springform pan.

In a large bowl using an electric mixer, beat the cream cheese until light and fluffy. Add the powdered sugar and beat until creamy. One at a time, add the eggs, beating well after each addition. Add the flour, vanilla, and lemon juice.

Pour the batter into the prepared springform pan and place the pan inside a larger roasting pan. Fill with hot water to come halfway up the sides of the pan. Place in the oven and bake for about 45 minutes, or until the top is golden and the cake is slightly firm.

Remove from the oven and place on a wire rack to cool completely. Cover and refrigerate for at least 6 hours or overnight.

Using a melon baller or small ice-cream scoop, form balls with the cheesecake and place on a cookie sheet lined with parchment paper. Insert a lollipop stick into each ball. Place in the freezer for at least 3 hours, or until the pops are totally frozen.

Melt the chocolate over a double boiler and stir to make a smooth sauce. Remove from the heat and cool to temper the chocolate. Dip each lollipop into the sauce and cover well on all sides. Decorate with sprinkles, chopped nuts, or candied fruit. Arrange the pops on a cookie sheet lined with parchment paper and return to the freezer until ready to serve.

BAREFOOT ON THE BOAT
KATHRYN AND LEO VECELLIO

NOTHING SAYS "WELCOME TO PALM BEACH" quite like the bevy of megayachts glittering alongside the Royal Palm Way bridge. Resplendent in white and powered to circumnavigate the globe—or at least to jaunt over to Capri and Monaco in the summer months, and perhaps down to St. Barths at Christmastime—these worldly vessels play host to some of the island's most highly coveted invitation-only events.

At the helm of the collection is the *Lady Kathryn III*, a 145-foot, Australian-built NQEA owned by Kathryn and Leo Vecellio and often enjoyed by their adult sons, Christopher and Michael. With interiors by Jack Fhillips and an art collection featuring the couple's favorite eighteenth- and nineteenth-century oils, one might easily mistake her stately salons and grand twenty-seven-beam design for those of a well-appointed island estate.

But when the Vecellios entertain friends, family, and colleagues, the mood aboard the *Lady Kathryn III* is elegantly casual. Guests kick off their shoes upon reaching the ship's entrance for cocktail receptions and dinner parties, while Captain Christopher Ramos and the crew greet everyone with warm smiles. After giving a hello kiss to their hosts in the main salon, guests are offered Champagne and cocktails via the al fresco bar on the aft deck before helping themselves to an abundant sushi bar outside the sky lounge. On the third level, plush cushions and flickering candles on the sun deck provide a comfortable meeting place for new friends and old as the sun sets behind the West Palm Beach skyline.

"We entertain in a very traditional, relaxed, and elegant style," Kathryn says. "We both love for our guests to really enjoy the food, service, presentation, and flower arrangements. After all these years I still plan, plan, and plan: The menu, seating arrangement, flowers, linens, and china are all very important to me. Taking care of everything in advance helps the host and hostess to be totally relaxed, and this in turn enables them to enjoy every second with their guests."

The family's favorite hors d'oeuvres—a no-fail combination of mini sliders, crab cakes, shumai, and other comfort foods—are passed at every party. "They are the ones that over many years are always crowd-pleasers," says Kathryn. "Sometimes the caterers or our chef will have a new recipe for me to try. If I love it, I will add it, but we rarely delete any past items. Tried and true go a long way."

TIPS AND IDEAS FROM
KATHRYN VECELLIO

Plan ahead so you can focus all of your attention on your guests.

Have plenty of candles (unscented) on hand. Decorate the entire room, not just the table, to create a warm atmosphere.

Have an abundance of beautiful flowers for the table, buffet, and to use throughout the room.

Use recipes that you trust and are crowd-pleasers.

Keep a well-stocked pantry for unexpected guests. Some no-fail combinations include: pâté and Brie cheese, fresh crackers, currant jelly, and whole dried fruit; smoked salmon (vacuum-packed or frozen) and caviar, fresh crackers, sour cream, capers, and onion; and frozen homemade blinis and lots of Champagne

Following grand cocktail receptions aboard the *Lady Kathryn III*, a close group of friends and family is often invited to stay for dinner in the dining room. For these occasions, she enjoys using her most beloved china patterns. "Henley by Minton was the first pattern I received as a new bride thirty-six years ago," she says. "I had many other patterns of china and sterling that I had inherited, but this was my first pattern of choice."

Christofle sterling silver, simple gold chargers, and gold-embellished Saint Louis Thistle crystal complement her treasured china atop place mats of delicate lace. "I love combining the elegance of the linens and crystals with the basic beauty of the wood table," she notes. "When my grandmother and mother entertained for a simple bridge party or for an elaborate Christmas dinner, I remember the delight in their eyes at being able to please their family and guests. Entertaining family and friends has been a much enjoyed multigenerational gift passed from mother to daughter."

MENU FOR FOUR

MINI-SLIDERS, CRAB CAKES, AND SHUMAI

SPRING GREEN SALAD WITH SLICED PEARS,
MAYTAG BLUE CHEESE, CANDIED PECANS,
AND RASPBERRY VINAIGRETTE

KATHYRN VECELLIO'S LOBSTER "RISOTTO"

ROASTED BEEF TENDERLOIN WITH BÉARNAISE SAUCE,
HARICOTS VERTS, ROASTED POTATOES,
AND **TOMATOES ROYALE**

FLOURLESS CHOCOLATE CAKE WITH CRÈME ANGLAISE

KATHYRN VECELLIO'S LOBSTER "RISOTTO"

This easy-to-make dish is reminiscent of Italian risotto but without the long cooking time and constant stirring. The flavor, as always, depends on the quality and freshness of the ingredients.

Serves 4

1	cup short-grain Valencia rice
3	cups chicken broth, preferably organic and low-sodium
2	tablespoons unsalted butter
1	medium Spanish onion, diced
½	teaspoon saffron threads
1	whole lobster tail, thawed if frozen, cooked and cut into slices
	Salt and freshly ground black pepper
½	cup grated Parmesan cheese

In a large saucepan, combine the rice with 2²/₃ cups of the chicken broth and bring to a boil over medium-high heat. Lower the heat, cover, and simmer for about 20 minutes, or until the rice is al dente. Toss with a fork and keep covered to keep warm.

In a small sauté pan, heat the butter over medium heat until melted. Add the onions and sauté until just translucent, 5 to 7 minutes, then stir them into the rice.

In a small bowl, add ¹/₃ cup of chicken broth. Crush the saffron with your fingers over the broth and let it dissolve. Add the chicken broth mixture to the rice and onion mixture.

Add the lobster meat to the rice mixture, reserving a slice of lobster for the garnish. Season with salt and pepper. Transfer to a serving bowl, sprinkle with the cheese, and garnish with the reserved lobster slice.

Top: Spring Green Salad;
Bottom: Kathryn Vecellio's Lobster "Risotto"

ROASTED BEEF TENDERLOIN WITH BÉARNAISE SAUCE

Tenderloin is the cut that filet mignon comes from. It is tender, delicious, and easy to carve, portion, and prepare. A side of béarnaise adds a special richness perfect for a celebratory dinner or Christmas feast.

Serves 4

1	(2-pound) beef tenderloin, trimmed of excess fat
	Salt and freshly ground black pepper
	Pinch of garlic powder
	Béarnaise Sauce (recipe follows)

Preheat the oven to 400°F.

Sprinkle the tenderloin with salt, pepper, and the garlic powder. Place on a flat roasting pan and bake for 20 minutes, or until a meat thermometer inserted in the thickest portion of the beef reads 140°F (medium to rare). Remove it from the oven, cover with aluminum foil or a kitchen towel, and let rest for 10 minutes before slicing. Serve with béarnaise sauce.

BÉARNAISE SAUCE

Makes about 1 1/2 cups

4	large egg yolks
1½	tablespoons fresh lemon juice
4	tablespoons (½ stick) unsalted butter, divided into 3 equal portions
¼	teaspoon salt
1	teaspoon chopped fresh tarragon
1	teaspoon chopped fresh flat-leaf parsley
1	tablespoon tarragon vinegar
1	teaspoon onion juice (from grating a piece of onion)
	Dash of ground cayenne

In the top portion of a double boiler, beat the egg yolks with the lemon juice. Add 1 portion of the butter, place over simmering water, and heat, stirring constantly, until the mixture begins to thicken. Remove from the heat, add the second portion of butter, and stir rapidly. Add the remaining butter and continue to stir until the mixture is completely blended. Add the remaining ingredients and return to the stovetop. Cook over moderate heat until thickened, about 3 to 4 minutes, stirring constantly. Serve immediately.

TOMATOES ROYALE

This easy, delicious recipe is a favorite in the Vecellio family, especially when accompanied by a beef tenderloin, but they also serve it with fish and chicken, and their vegetarian guests enjoy it solo.

Serves 4

4	medium ripe but firm tomatoes, cut in half
2	teaspoons dried basil
2	teaspoons salt
3	tablespoons minced green bell pepper
	Pinch of garlic powder
1	cup shredded Parmesan cheese
½	cup mayonnaise

Preheat the oven to 425°F.

Place each tomato half, cut side up, in a 6-inch square of aluminum foil and place on an ungreased baking sheet.

Combine the remaining ingredients in a medium bowl and spoon the mixture over the tomato halves.

Place in the oven and bake for about 10 minutes, until the tomatoes begin to soften and the cheese melts. Serve immediately.

FLOURLESS CHOCOLATE CAKE

The Vecellios's cake is delicious floating in crème anglaise; dedicated chocolate lovers have the option of drizzling chocolate sauce atop the cake in place of the crème anglaise.

Makes 1 (9-inch) cake; serves 6

10½	ounces semisweet or dark chocolate, chopped
1	cup (2 sticks) unsalted butter, cut into pieces
6	large eggs, at room temperature
	Pinch of salt
	Crème Anglaise (recipe follows) for serving
	Powdered sugar, for dusting

Preheat the oven to 350°F and butter a 9-inch springform pan.

In a double boiler, melt the chocolate and butter, stirring until smooth. Remove from the heat and cool.

In a large bowl using an electric mixer, beat the eggs and salt at a very high speed until tripled in volume and fluffy. Using a spatula, fold the chocolate into the eggs.

Pour the batter into the prepared pan, place in the oven, and bake for 15 to 20 minutes, or until the center is almost firm but still jiggles a bit when you move it. The cake will continue to cook as it cools. Remove from the oven and cool the cake in the pan on a wire rack.

Invert the cake onto a platter, spoon crème anglaise onto dessert plates, and place a slice of cake at the center of each. Dust with powdered sugar. (Alternatively, you can invert the cake onto a decorative platter, sprinkle with powdered sugar, and bring it to the table with crème anglaise on the side.)

CRÈME ANGLAISE

Makes 3 cups

6	large egg yolks
2	tablespoons sugar
2	cups half-and-half
1	teaspoon vanilla extract

In a large metal bowl and using a handheld electric mixer, beat the egg yolks and sugar until light and fluffy.

In a medium saucepan, warm the half-and-half with the vanilla over low heat.

Place the metal bowl over a pan of simmering water and, in a stream, whisk in the warm half-and-half with the egg mixture. Using a wooden spoon, stir constantly until the custard has thickened, about 4 to 5 minutes. Place the metal bowl over an ice-water bath to stop the cooking; stir until completely cooled, then cover and refrigerate until ready to serve.

TASTEMAKERS
ENTERTAINING WITH STYLE

DINNER IS IN THE DETAILS
KARA AND STEVE ROSS

DINNER WITH STEVE AND KARA ROSS is an evening filled with warmth and genuine friendship, fascinating conversation, and lots of belly laughs. The Rosses are busy people—Steve is founder, chairman, and CEO of the Related Companies and owns the Miami Dolphins football franchise; Kara is the founder of Kara Ross New York, a luxury accessories company—so their days are packed with travel, business meetings, trunk shows, appearances, football games, family time, and a whirlwind social schedule. Downtime is precious and is often spent at home.

Dining at home affords the Rosses an opportunity to eat healthfully and enjoy their guests in a relaxed environment. Their Treanor & Fatio–designed oceanfront home, considered the best design of Maurice Fatio's career, was built in 1936 and serves as the perfect refuge to host any gathering.

When planning a dinner, the Rosses usually begin with the guest list. "Steve and I think of people we like to spend time with, or friends we haven't seen in a while," says Kara. "We consider who those friends might enjoy seeing, or who they don't know but may enjoy meeting, and the guest list grows."

For the menu, the Rosses rely on Angel Burbano, their personal chef. Because Steve likes healthful food such as salads, fish, and vegetables, Chef Angel begins with a wealth of fresh ingredients and adds his own flavorful twist.

Kara feels passionately about designing the tablescape. "I create the table much like I design a piece of jewelry," she says. "I start with a color or an idea and begin layering, mixing, and matching. Creating a beautiful table shows guests you put some time and effort into creating an ambiance. The table sets a tone for the evening, more so than the food."

The table design is often "built around a found object." For this party, inspiration has come from a piece of driftwood. Kara has gathered glass water tubes, wrapped them in raffia, glued them to the willowy branches, and filled them with colorful flowers. This stunningly easy-to-make centerpiece with its striking shapes and textures sparks conversations about design and travel, without hindering guests' ability to chat across the table.

Think of the table as a blank canvas. Use your favorite things to decorate—objects you've collected over the years. What you create is your own personal work of art.

The table setting is the backdrop for the food that will be served, so always think of the table first.

Be creative, fun, playful. Mix and match. It shows your guests you've spent time thinking about them and the evening.

I *love* my good friend Kim Seybert's tabletop fashions—definitely the best on the market.

Some of my favorite tabletop finds have come from flea markets and antique shows, and fun things that I've collected during my travels.

Candies! Candies can add the right punch of color. Pour them into a favorite bowl.

Don't forget a dinner party is really just about good friends coming over for dinner—so nothing should be too serious or stiff. It is supposed to be fun, and I try and make it just that.

For an interesting backdrop, a bolt of neutral-toned ikat fabric is draped over the table. Lotus bowls discovered in India are filled with bright yellow candies, adding a pop of color to the table. For a touch of tactile luxury, Kara has introduced pieces from Kim Seybert's line of tabletop fashions. The table is warm and sunny, the breeze blows lightly, and dusk settles on the ocean's edge.

As guests approach the table, the sun sets, conversations shift, and the cheerful sound of laughter can be heard. The manzanita branch on the table sparks talk of Kara's recent creation of wooden cuffs from a magnolia tree on the White House lawn—jewelry for the first lady to present to visiting heads of state and departing female staffers. Talk swiftly shifts to football and Steve's recent trip abroad.

The ambiance the Rosses have created causes guests to linger. Old friendships are revisited and new ones made, ideas are shared, and everyone agrees it is a picture-perfect evening in Palm Beach.

MOJITO

This popular summer cocktail is refreshing year-round in the balmy Palm Beach climate. Made of five ingredients, its combination creates the right balance of sweetness, refreshing citrus, and spearmint flavors. Blending the flavors is key.

Makes 1 drink

2   tablespoons simple syrup

Generous pinch of fresh mint leaves

1   lime, cut into quarters

2   ounces clear rum, preferably aged Cuban rum (Bacardi Superior Light works well too)

Club soda

Lime wedge, mint sprig, and sugar cane swizzle stick for serving

To make simple syrup, combine equal parts water and sugar in a saucepan over medium heat. Heat until the sugar dissolves. To make enough for a party, combine 3 cups water with 3 cups sugar to yield about 4 cups. Keep refrigerated until ready to use.

Muddle the mint leaves and lime quarters in the bottom of a tall mojito glass, cocktail shaker, or mixing receptacle. (You can also muddle a pinch of sugar with the mint and lime to extract the lime's essential oils.)

Add ice to fill the glass, then add simple syrup and rum. The glass should be about three quarters full. Shake or stir until fully blended. Transfer to a serving glass and top with club soda. Garnish with a lime wedge, mint sprig, and sugar cane swizzle stick.

ANGEL'S GAZPACHO SHOTS

While this soup would make a wonderful first course, the Rosses chose to serve it as an hors d'oeuvre presented in shot glasses. Fun, unexpected, and delicious.

Makes 6 bowls or 12 to 15 "shots"

1½	pounds vine-ripened tomatoes, peeled, seeded, and chopped
6	cups tomato juice
1	cup peeled, seeded, and chopped cucumber
½	cup cored, seeded, and chopped red bell pepper
½	cup chopped red onion
1	medium clove garlic, minced
¼	cup extra-virgin olive oil
	Juice of 1 lime
2	teaspoons balsamic vinegar
2	teaspoons Worcestershire sauce
1	teaspoon salt
¼	teaspoon freshly ground black pepper
2	tablespoons chopped fresh basil
	Parsley
	Tabasco sauce, to taste (optional)
	Sour cream for garnish
	Buckwheat shoots for garnish

Place all the ingredients in a blender and blend well, just like a smoothie. Garnish each bowl or shot with a little sour cream and a buckwheat shoot.

TRICOLOR SALAD

The key to perfecting this salad is to cut all the ingredients to even, bite-size pieces; it just adds to the visual impact. You can also assemble the salad in individual 3-inch round molds for an impressive presentation.

Serves 6

1	cup peeled, diced seedless cucumber
1	pint cherry tomatoes, halved
5	large strawberries, hulled and diced
½	cup kalamata olives, halved and pitted
1	whole avocado, peeled, pitted, and diced
1	yellow bell pepper, cored, seeded, and diced
	Raspberry Vinaigrette (recipe follows)
5	to 6 ounces arugula or mixed greens
½	cup crumbled Gorgonzola cheese
½	cup caramelized pecan halves

In a large bowl, toss together the cucumber, tomatoes, strawberries, olives, avocado, and yellow pepper. Dress with ¾ cup of raspberry vinaigrette.

In a medium bowl, toss the arugula with the remaining ¼ cup of vinaigrette.

To serve, divide the arugula among 6 plates, top with the vegetable and fruit mixture, and garnish with the cheese and pecans.

RASPBERRY VINAIGRETTE

Makes 3 cups

½	cup extra-virgin olive oil
½	cup raspberry vinegar
1	pint raspberries
	Juice of 4 small lemons (about ¾ cup)
	Salt and freshly ground black pepper

In a blender, combine the olive oil, vinegar, raspberries, and lemon juice and blend until smooth. Season with salt and pepper. Chill for at least one hour before serving; it will keep overnight. Leftover dressing can be stored in the refrigerator for up to 3 days. For a casual lunch, use it to create a fruity spinach salad topped with walnuts and fresh raspberries.

ANGEL'S CHILEAN SEA BASS WITH FRESH HERBS AND HONEY-MUSTARD SAUCE

This easy, delicious recipe also works well with halibut.

Serves 6

½	cup extra-virgin olive oil
3	cloves garlic, diced
5	tablespoons thinly sliced fresh basil
5	tablespoons finely chopped fresh flat-leaf parsley
2	shallots, thinly sliced
	Salt and freshly ground black pepper
6	(5- to 6-ounce) Chilean sea bass fillets
½	cup dry white wine, preferably Pinot Grigio
	Honey-Mustard Sauce (recipe follows)
	Mango Salsa (store-bought) for garnish
	Aged Balsamic Vinegar to drizzle

Preheat the oven to 400°F and oil a large baking dish.

In a medium bowl, mix together the olive oil, garlic, basil, parsley, and shallots to make an herb marinade. Season with salt and pepper and set aside.

In a dry sauté pan over high heat, sear the sea bass fillets on both sides until the edges turn slightly golden, about 3 minutes per side. Arrange the fillets in the prepared baking dish and cover with the marinade. Drizzle with the wine.

Place in the oven and bake for 15 to 20 minutes, or until the fish is cooked through and flakes easily when pierced with a fork. To serve, arrange the fillets on a serving platter, spooning any sauce on top. Top with honey-mustard sauce, garnish with mango salsa, and drizzle with aged balsamic vinegar. Serve immediately.

HONEY-MUSTARD SAUCE

Makes 1 cup

¼	cup mayonnaise
1	tablespoon Dijon-style mustard
1	tablespoon honey
2	tablespoons fresh lemon juice
2	tablespoons finely chopped fresh flat-leaf parsley
2	tablespoons finely chopped fresh rosemary
	Salt and freshly ground black pepper

In a small bowl, whisk together the mayonnaise, mustard, honey, lemon juice, parsley, and rosemary. Season with salt and pepper. Transfer to a small saucepan and warm over low heat, stirring often.

To serve, transfer to a sauceboat and pass at the table.

GARLIC MASHED POTATOES

Serves 6

6	large russet potatoes, peeled and cubed
4	cloves garlic, peeled
½	cup (1 stick) unsalted butter, cut into chunks
1	cup milk
	Salt and freshly ground black pepper

Fill a large saucepan with water and add salt; add the potatoes and garlic, bring to a boil, then reduce the heat and simmer for 20 minutes, or until the potatoes are very soft and easily pierced with a fork.

Drain the water, add the butter and milk, and, using a whisk, mash the potatoes until fluffy. Season with salt and pepper. If not serving immediately, warm over low heat just before serving.

Top left: Angel's Chilean Sea Bass; Top right: Cheese and Blueberries; Bottom: Prosciutto-wrapped Asparagus

Preheat the oven to 350°F.

In a food processor, pulse together the biscuits and almonds. In a stream, add the melted butter through the feed tube and pulse until it resembles wet sand. Divide the mixture into 6 round tartlet pans and press with your fingers to create a shell. Place in the freezer for at least 2 hours to set. (If you don't wish to make the crust, you can purchase ready-made graham-cracker-crust shells.)

In a medium bowl, combine the condensed milk, egg yolks, lime juice, and 1 teaspoon of the lime zest; mix well. Pour the mixture into the prepared shells.

In a medium bowl using an electric mixer, beat the egg whites with the cream of tartar until thick and stiff. Add the powdered sugar and continue whipping until glossy. Add the remaining 1 teaspoon lime zest and mix well.

Spoon the meringue on top of the Key lime ramekins, completely covering the crust. Place in the oven and bake for about 10 minutes, or until the tops are golden. Remove from the oven and place on wire racks to cool completely; cover and refrigerate until chilled. Serve cold.

To serve, remove the pies from the pans and garnish each with a slice of lime.

INDIVIDUAL KEY LIME PIES

Adapted from a favorite Paula Deen recipe, Angel has created a more delicate individual pie. Great for dinner parties or a ladies' lunch.

Makes 6 individual pies

1½	cups crumbled whole wheat biscuits, such as Carr's Whole Wheat Crackers
½	cup thinly sliced almonds
½	cup (1 stick) unsalted butter, melted
1	(14-ounce) can sweetened condensed milk
2	large eggs, separated
½	cup Key lime juice
2	teaspoons lime zest
¼	teaspoon cream of tartar
¼	cup powdered sugar
6	lime slices for garnish

Opposite:
Chef Angel Burbano

ON THE TERRACE
ARNOLD SCAASI AND PARKER LADD

ARNOLD SCAASI AND PARKER LADD have enjoyed fifty years of loving friendship filled with exciting careers, exotic travel, fascinating friends, and lots and lots of parties. Whether hosting a dinner in Manhattan, cocktails at their beloved Le Cirque, a gathering in Quogue, or a dinner party here in Palm Beach, when friends open a hand-written invitation, monogrammed SCAALADD, they know they are invited to an unforgettable celebration filled with delicious food and illustrious guests.

As you drive up to their Mediterranean-style home in Palm Beach, there is a festive excitement in the air. The doors open to a dramatic red entryway; friends are greeted with a warm welcome and immediately feel like they have arrived in a very special place as they are floated past the Venetian room and onto the terrace, where introductions are made.

For Arnold and Parker, people are the most important element of a party. "We aim for a crowd that will get along with each other," Arnold says. "Once in a while, it's interesting to interject a new person who others may not know."

The setting has been created just as meticulously as the guest list. Being seated on the terrace banquette is a dreamy experience, where guests are surrounded by brilliantly colored Scaasi pillows in a "room" accessorized as beautifully as some of his best-dressed clients.

After cocktails and hors d'oeuvres, guests are escorted to dinner inside. Arnold loves to set the table—and the mood. He usually begins with place mats from his collection—he has more than two hundred sets, sourced around the world—but for this party he chooses a tablecloth that works like a canvas for the coral-patterned Limoges china and filigree glasses from Pier I.

He loves to mix fine and fun objects, insisting that provenance does not matter. "There are no rules," he says. "The only rule is to make the table attractive."

His eye is so practiced that he does that intuitively. Instead of flowers, which he does not care to use on the table, he uses collected objects as a centerpiece. Tonight two silver

Plan your guest list carefully. That is the most important element of the evening.

Save fresh flowers for other rooms; don't put them on the table. Decorate with your favorite objects; it is so much more interesting. Make the table attractive. When guests come to the table and find it cheerful and attractive, it sets the mood for dinner conversation.

Set the table beautifully every time, even if it is a dinner for two.

Make the foods guests will enjoy. Good-quality, simple foods are best. Nothing overly complicated. We have been serving chicken pot pie for years, and our guests look forward to having it. When friends are invited to dinner they request Glen's gnocchi (page 160).

elephants grace the table, along with a few branches of the bougainvillea blooming in the garden.

Glendina Weste, who has been with Arnold and Parker for more than thirty-five years, enters in a crisp, white Scaasi-designed uniform and greets guests affectionately as she surveys the room, ensuring that everyone is well cared for. Her cooking is legendary in Palm Beach. Her spinach gnocchi, served tonight, leaves everyone speechless. She's also famous for her shortbread cookies, which are based on a recipe passed down from Parker's grandmother.

Arnold keeps a buzzer near his place setting so he can alert the kitchen if a dish or glass needs refilling; this way he never has to leave his guests. After all, the host should enjoy the evening too.

The dapper elegance with which Arnold and Parker entertain is reminiscent of an earlier time, when following the established traditions of refined society and exhibiting good taste was still very much in fashion. After a dinner party, they will expect a call from you the next day to chat about memories of the evening, ask if you met anyone interesting, and, of course, to make plans for another gathering.

GLEN'S SPINACH AND RICOTTA GNOCCHI

Glen prefers to use frozen spinach for her famous gnocchi, but you can use fresh and cook it the same way—just be sure to squeeze it as dry as possible.

Serves 6

1	cup (2 sticks) unsalted butter
3	pounds chopped frozen spinach, thawed
6	large eggs
	Dash of grated nutmeg
1	pound ricotta cheese
3	cups grated Parmesan cheese
2	cups all-purpose flour, plus more for dusting
	Salt and freshly ground black pepper

In a large sauté pan, melt ½ cup of the butter over medium heat. Add the spinach and cook until it releases all its liquid. Transfer to a colander to drain, pressing with the back of a spoon to squeeze out as much liquid as possible. Set aside to cool.

In a large bowl, beat the eggs with the nutmeg, ricotta cheese, 2 cups of the Parmesan cheese, and the flour. Season with salt and pepper. Add the spinach and mix well. The dough should be sticky but not wet; add more flour if needed. Spread the mixture onto a large baking sheet and let dry completely, or until cool enough to handle.

Sprinkle a layer of flour onto a cutting board. Take spoonfuls of the spinach-ricotta mixture and form into croquette shapes, the size of a large dessert spoon, and roll them in the flour.

Bring a large pot of salted water to boil and drop the gnocchi in, 10 to 12 at a time. When they float to the surface, after 2 or 3 minutes, remove them with a slotted spoon, drain well, and arrange on a decorative broiler-safe baking dish.

When you are ready to serve the gnocchi, preheat the broiler. Melt the remaining ½ cup of butter in a small saucepan and pour it over the gnocchi. Sprinkle with the remaining 1 cup of Parmesan cheese, place under the broiler, and broil for 3 to 5 minutes, or until the top is golden and the gnocchi are heated through. Serve immediately.

PORK LOIN ROAST

The pork will need to marinate for at least six hours, so plan accordingly.

Serves 6

1	cup extra-virgin olive oil
½	cup fresh thyme leaves
½	cup fresh rosemary
1	cup soy sauce
1	teaspoon ground black pepper
1	(5- to 6-pound) pork loin, trimmed
	Glen's Stuffing (recipe follows)

Glen's Spinach and Ricotta
Gnocchi; Pork Loin Roast and
Glen's stuffing

In a roasting pan, whisk together the olive oil, thyme, rosemary, soy sauce, and black pepper to make a marinade. Place the pork loin in the marinade, cover, and refrigerate for at least 6 hours and up to 8 hours, turning once.

Preheat the oven to 325°F.

Place the pork loin in the oven and bake for about 3 hours (30 minutes per pound).

Remove the meat from the pan and let it rest, covered, for about 10 minutes for the juices to reabsorb. Strain the pan liquid into a clean pot, bring to a boil, then reduce the heat and simmer until the liquid reduces by half. Taste and adjust the seasoning if needed.

To serve, cut the pork into thin slices and pour some of the gravy on top. Pass the rest of the gravy in a sauceboat at the table, along with the stuffing.

GLEN'S STUFFING

This easy-to-make stuffing gives guests the feeling they are home, creating a warm, welcoming atmosphere at dinner.

Serves 6

1	large onion, chopped
	Pinch of fresh thyme leaves
½	cup minced celery
1	tablespoon roughly chopped fresh flat-leaf parsley
2	cups chicken stock, preferably low-sodium
1	(14-ounce) bag herb-seasoned stuffing, such as Pepperidge Farm
	Salt and freshly ground black pepper

In a large pan, combine the onion, thyme, celery, parsley, and chicken stock. Place over medium heat and bring to a simmer, about 8 minutes. Stir in the stuffing and season with salt and pepper. Keep covered and warm until ready to serve.

FRUIT COMPOTE

Serves 6

1	(16-ounce) can black cherries
1	(16-ounce) can peach halves, drained
1	(16-ounce) box dried apricots
	Juice of 1 orange
	Juice of 1 lemon
½	cup packed brown sugar
1	unpeeled orange, sliced
1	unpeeled lemon, sliced
	Sour cream, ice cream, or yogurt for serving

Preheat the oven to 350°F.

In a 9-inch souffle dish or oven-to-table decorative casserole, combine the cherries and their juice, the drained peaches, and the apricots. Add the orange and lemon juices and brown sugar and mix well. Arrange the orange and lemon slices on top. Place in the oven and bake for 2 hours, or until the fruit is very soft (it will be the consistency of a very thick jam or marmalade). Serve hot or cold, with a dollop of sour cream, ice cream, or yogurt on top.

SCAALADD'S SHORTBREAD COOKIES

This recipe is a Ladd family favorite and was passed down to Parker from his grandmother. Arnold styled the cookies by making them into small rounds that fit perfectly at the bottom of his compote dishes and also sit beautifully atop a silver tray for passing at the table.

Makes 30 cookies

4	sticks (1 pound) unsalted butter, at room temperature
½	cup powdered sugar
½	cup packed brown sugar
2¾	cups all-purpose flour
¾	cup cornstarch
½	teaspoon baking powder

Preheat the oven to 325°F and line a baking sheet with parchment paper.

In a large bowl using an electric mixer on medium speed, cream the butter with the powdered and brown sugars until fluffy.

Sift the flour, cornstarch, and baking powder into the bowl. Mix well to make a firm dough. Transfer to a well-floured work surface and roll the dough out about ¼ inch thick with a rolling pin or your hands. Using a 1- to 2-inch cookie cutter, cut the dough into shapes and transfer to the prepared baking sheet.

Place in the oven and bake for about 20 minutes, until golden. Transfer the cookies to a wire rack to cool completely. Serve on a decorative platter to be passed or include 2 as an accompaniment to servings of the fruit compote.

Glendina Weste

Fruit Compote with
SCAALADD's Shortbread Cookies

DINNER BY DESIGN
LARS BOLANDER
AND NADINE KALACHNIKOFF

THERE IS PERHAPS NO BETTER EXAMPLE of the ideal balance between a fearless sense of style and the comfort and ease of Palm Beach living than at the West Palm Beach home of Nadine Kalachnikoff and internationally acclaimed interior designer Lars Bolander. Here, a playful yet precisely placed collection of nineteenth-century antiques and ethnic artifacts collected during their thirty-year marriage highlights a life well lived.

But there is one thing you will not find at this globally inspired retreat: a dining room.

"It's a waste of space," says Lars, snuggled up with Nadine on a deep sofa in a living room peppered with books, family photos, and comfy places to perch. "A lot of people in Palm Beach have help and kitchen staff, which we don't have here. It's much more fun without staff. Otherwise it can be rather stiff."

Dinner parties begin with poolside drinks in the garden pavilion (Nadine loves to mix a great cocktail), followed by dinner at the kitchen table. "I don't care if it's the president of the United States, he's going to get up and put dishes in the kitchen sink," says Nadine with a laugh. If the best parties end up in the kitchen, you can imagine the fun to be had when one begins there.

Both Lars and Nadine, who manage design studios and antique shops in Midtown Manhattan and West Palm Beach's Antique Row, love to cook—he, influenced by the traditional Scandinavian holiday smorgasbords of his childhood; she, by the soulful meals of Spanish paella and savory Russian soups prepared with her parents and sisters when growing up in New York. But they always take turns preparing meals. "We don't cook together, because then we argue," Nadine says with a wry smile.

"Cooking is very relaxing," says Lars. "It's like painting. You don't think about anything else but what you're going to do." It is perhaps this relaxed tone that lends invaluable intimacy to guests' experience in their home, ensuring that an invitation to dinner is seldom declined.

If you love to make drinks, be sure to incorporate them into your evening. Have fun with seasonal finds; if fresh peaches are available I'll serve them with Myers's rum and lemon juice or whatever strikes me.

Life is too short to drink bad wine, but it doesn't have to be outrageously expensive. Buy in advance and stock up on favorites, like the lovely rioja Spanish wines found at Costco.

When planning your dinner, think of the five senses, and appeal to all of them.

Decorate your table beautifully.

Choose music appropriate to the mood.

Prepare delicious foods; use your trusted recipes.

Use fresh ingredients, aromatic spices, and fresh herbs.

Create a tactile experience with table linens, chopsticks, or an unusually shaped glass.

Guests seated in the expansive kitchen have a view to the open butler's pantry, stacked high with everything from Herend to handmade, and the couple's vast library of cookbooks from around the world. "Having been to Bali and Burma and all those countries, I think the entertaining there is so extraordinary," says Nadine, also a former caterer and mother of two adult sons. "The food is simple, very clean, and absolutely delicious. They are very visual. They just don't put pasta in the middle of the plate—you eat with your eyes."

At a dark wood kitchen table surrounded by white director's chairs, Nadine sets a mélange of fragrant fresh herb centerpieces, Chinese figurines, and dishes from New York and Bali. The three-course Asian dinner is a tribute to friends preparing to leave for New York and Los Angeles for the summer.

"When you set a table like that, it's like a gift," she says. "You don't use the same glass and the same plate and the same fork and knife. You try to use all your senses—the music, the smells, everything. People see that you've taken time for them, and it's not the maid who's set the table and that's it."

VIETNAMESE VEGETABLE SUMMER ROLLS

The filling for these rolls is a quick and tasty way to pickle vegetables, and it is easy to make a big batch; the pickled vegetables can be stored in the refrigerator for several weeks and used in salads or to garnish other dishes. Slice the summer rolls in two for appetizer portions at a seated dinner, or cut into 1-inch pieces and serve as passed hors d'oeuvres. Slice at a 45-degree angle to elevate the presentation and show off the fresh ingredients inside.

Serves 6

3	large carrots, julienned
1	medium daikon, julienned
1	large red onion, julienned
1	large unpeeled cucumber, cut in half, seeded, and julienned
1	cup Japanese rice wine vinegar
1/3	cup sugar
2	tablespoons salt
12	rice paper rolls
12	small Thai basil leaves

Arrange the carrots, daikon, red onion, and cucumber in a shallow bowl.

In a small saucepan, combine the vinegar, sugar, salt, and $^1/_3$ cup of water. Place over medium heat and bring to a boil, stirring to dissolve the sugar and salt. Pour over the vegetables and cool to room temperature. Drain the vegetables, dry them, and set aside.

Working with one rice paper roll at a time, dip a roll in a bowl filled with warm water and place on a cutting board (you can spray the cutting board with nonstick cooking spray to make your work easier). Lay a group of the vegetables and a basil leaf in the bottom third of the rice paper, fold in the bottom and sides, and roll tightly. The paper will stick to itself, creating a seal. Slice and serve.

THAI VERMICELLI SALAD WITH SHRIMP AND FRESH HERBS

You can also use chicken or tofu in place of the shrimp for equally delicious results.

Serves 6

5	ounces vermicelli noodles
2	tablespoons fish sauce
¼	cup fresh lime juice
1	tablespoon sugar
1	tablespoon minced fresh ginger
½	cup grapeseed oil
1	cup julienned mixed herbs, such as basil, Thai basil, cilantro, and mint
1½	pounds cooked medium shrimp (about 4 per serving)
½	cup canola oil, plus more for frying
¼	cup all-purpose flour
2	medium shallots, sliced into rounds

Prepare the noodles according to the package instructions. Drain, pat dry, and set aside.

In a large bowl, whisk together the fish sauce, lime juice, sugar, ginger, and grapeseed oil; stir to dissolve the sugar. Add the herbs and toss in the vermicelli and shrimp.

In a medium skillet, heat ½ inch of oil over medium-high heat. Place the flour in a shallow bowl, dust the shallots with flour, and, working in batches, fry the shallots until golden brown. Place on a paper towel–lined plate to drain.

To serve, toss the salad well and top with the fried shallots.

KOREAN BO SAMM (SLOW-ROASTED PORK SHOULDER) LETTUCE WRAPS

Serves 6

½	cup salt
¼	cup granulated sugar
1	(5- to 6-pound) pork shoulder or Boston butt
¼	cup packed brown sugar
12	whole Bibb or Boston lettuce leaves
	Sliced vegetables, such as scallions, cucumbers, carrots, and daikon, for serving
	Condiments and sauces, such as hoisin sauce, fish sauce, Korean barbecue sauce, and/or spicy Thai chile vinaigrette, for serving

Combine the salt and granulated sugar in a small bowl. Rub the pork with the mixture, place in a plastic bag, and marinate in the refrigerator overnight.

Preheat the oven to 300°F. Take the pork out of the refrigerator about 30 minutes before placing in the oven so it can come to room temperature. Rinse the pork and pat dry. Place the pork in a small roasting pan fat side up and roast for 1 hour, then lower the oven temperature to 250°F and continue roasting for 3 more hours.

In a small saucepan, combine the brown sugar with ¼ cup of water. Place over medium heat and heat, stirring, until the brown sugar dissolves. Pour over the pork and continue roasting for another hour, or until the meat is easily shredded when pulled apart from the bone.

Remove from the oven and let the pork rest until it is cool enough to handle, then shred it using two forks and spoon any pan juices on top. To serve, arrange the lettuce leaves and sliced vegetables alongside the pork on a decorative plate and instruct your guests to assemble their wraps. Serve with your choice of condiments and sauces.

A COLLECTOR'S ENCHANTED EVENING
BETH RUDIN DEWOODY

AT "THE FIFTIES HOUSE" ON Palm Beach's Intracoastal Waterway, time on the oversize carriage clock seems to stand still in contrast to everything around it.

Entering Beth Rudin DeWoody's home on party night is like entering an enchanted world. Guests are surrounded by riotous color expressed in neon signs, glimmering glass collections, a birch-tree forest in a box; art is everywhere, often in the most unexpected places. Even at the bar, a simple pour becomes a mesmerizing piece of performance art. You don't know where art ends and life begins. Is that drink the barman just poured marked "Drink Me?" Is the faint smell of chocolate foreshadowing a story about to be told?

The question marks are part of the experience. Beth loves to surprise and to provoke— all in the name of creating memories. "Guests should feel the evening was fun and their visit worthwhile," she says. "I want people to go away feeling that they had a great time, met interesting people, enjoyed the art, even if they don't like everything, and enjoyed how it's put together."

She has been known to place an important, rare piece of art next to a flea market find, creating an atmosphere that guests find relaxing and comfortable, yet still have the sense they are being pampered by one of Palm Beach's most remarkable hostesses.

An array of artistically created fare is set out on a grand buffet table. The placement of food mimics a painting nearby, causing guests to wonder which came first. Of the food, Beth says, "I know what I like, and I know music. I like to focus on the ideas and concepts that pull the evening together."

The beauty of her parties is the seamless way in which those concepts come together; so seamless, in fact, that guests feel like they are part of the picture. Where there are pockets of silence, guests find video art on a big screen, an installation that demands quiet contemplation, or a marionette performing burlesque. The guest craving a little eighties fun need only step into the "Porta Party" for an experience in time travel—close the door and you are instantly transported to Studio 54. Everywhere guests turn, there is something wonderful to behold; some magical, others confounding.

A party is an opportunity to share my collection, my home, and my friends. Sharing my vision with other people and helping an institution I care about at the same time is a reason to celebrate.

Use your collection to style the table—glass catches the light nicely.

Tables are fun when they are colorful and crowded.

Flowers are not a must on the table.

Don't use scented candles.

Serve good food that you know people will enjoy. Who doesn't like chocolate cake?

Even if you have an abundance of staff, guests feel uncomfortable if someone is hovering over an empty glass or empty plate. Encourage them to help themselves or flag down the staff if they prefer.

Guests should go away feeling that they had a great time, met interesting people, and enjoyed the art. They should feel it was worthwhile to come.

Dinner is an equally artistic experience. Some dining tables are round, others square or oval, but all are colorful and crowded with Beth's collection of paperweights and vintage glasses, along with other found objects. She says, "I am a hopeless collector. Even before I had the house, I'd go up and down Dixie Highway, visiting all the dealers there. Almost everything here is from West Palm—and a few things from Miami; all of it is local. It is important to preserve the home by collecting in the period; every piece has a story, or meaning to me."

Indeed, the home, a work of art itself, is filled with an impressive mix of mid-twentieth-century furniture, a fascinating collection of artifacts, photography, books, and vintage clothing, all arranged with the precision and skilled eye of a great curator.

The only thing Beth loves more than her fifties house is sharing it with friends. She says, "Having a party gives me the chance to share my vision with other people." Her vision for this evening is not just her exceptional art, but delicious cuisine and intimate conversation.

As the evening progresses, the chocolate cake arrives. It is the denouement to a great story that is a cross between a classic and fairy tale.

SANGRIA

Serves 12

2	whole oranges, sliced
2	whole lemons, sliced
2	large peaches, peeled, pitted, and diced
2	medium plums, peeled, pitted, and diced
2	cups strawberries, hulled and sliced
3	large apples, peeled, cored, and sliced
¼	cup sugar
½	cup vodka
2	(750-ml) bottles white or red wine
1	cup fresh mint leaves

In a pitcher, mix together the oranges, lemons, peaches, plums, strawberries, and apples. Add the sugar and toss. Add the vodka and wine and stir. Chill. To serve, garnish the glasses with mint leaves.

SMOKED SALMON DIP

Makes 2 cups

4	ounces smoked salmon
½	cup mayonnaise
2	tablespoons mild extra-virgin olive oil
2	tablespoons honey
	Pinch of salt
1	tablespoon Dijon-style mustard
2	tablespoons roughly chopped fresh cilantro
4	ounces cream cheese, softened
1	tablespoon fresh lemon juice
½	medium yellow onion, diced

In a food processor, combine all the ingredients and pulse until pureed. Transfer to a decorative dish, cover, and refrigerate until ready to serve. Serve with crackers and crudités.

One of Palm Beach's most popular bartenders, Michael Lawrence.

WHOLE POACHED SALMON

Poached salmon is perfect for a big crowd, and it can be made ahead and kept in the refrigerator overnight. If the salmon is too long to fit into your fish poacher, you may cut off the head and tail, although the presentation is more impressive with the entire fish intact.

Serves 12

- 1 (7-pound) whole wild salmon, gutted and scaled with head and tail intact
- Salt and freshly ground black pepper
- ¾ cup fresh tarragon leaves
- 2 tablespoons extra-virgin olive oil
- 2 cups chopped onions
- 1 cup chopped carrots
- 1 cup chopped celery
- 1 bouquet garni (bay leaves, oregano, rosemary, and tarragon, about ¼ cup of each, wrapped in cheesecloth and tied with kitchen string)
- 4 cups dry white wine
- 4 cups fresh fish stock or chicken broth
- 1 large unpeeled seedless cucumber, thinly sliced
- Juice of 1 lemon
- Toast points

Season the fish with salt, pepper, and tarragon, making sure to season the inside of the fish as well. Place on a large baking sheet and refrigerate for 3 to 4 hours.

Preheat the oven to 350°F.

Heat the olive oil in a large sauté pan over medium heat. Add the onions, carrots, and celery and sauté until softened, about 10 to 12 minutes. Season with salt and pepper.

Place the sautéed vegetables and bouquet garni at the bottom of a fish poacher. Place the fish on the rack of the poacher and put the rack in place on top of the vegetable mixture. Pour the wine and stock over the fish, covering it completely in the liquid. Cover the poacher, place in the oven, and bake for 45 minutes, or until the fish is cooked through.

Remove the fish, let it cool, then refrigerate for at least 1 hour or overnight. Before serving, remove the skin from the top of the fish. Using the back of a paring knife, gently scrape off any brown fat. Cover the fish completely with the cucumber slices, arranging them in overlapping layers to resemble fish scales. Serve cold.

CHOCOLATE BUNDT CAKE

Makes 1 large cake; serves 12

- 1 box Duncan Hines Moist Deluxe Devil's Food Cake Mix
- 1 (5-ounce) Jell-O Instant Chocolate Pudding Mix
- 4 large eggs, beaten
- ½ cup vegetable oil
- 16 ounces sour cream
- 12 ounces semisweet chocolate chips

Preheat the oven to 350°F and butter a Bundt pan.

In a large bowl, mix the cake mix with the chocolate pudding mix. Using a spatula, fold in the eggs, then vegetable oil, ½ cup of water, and sour cream. Add chocolate chips and combine thoroughly.

Pour the batter into the prepared Bundt pan, place in the oven, and bake for 50 minutes, or until the edges begin to separate from the pan and a skewer comes out clean when inserted into the center of the cake. Remove from the oven, cool completely on a wire rack, then invert onto a decorative plate, slice, and serve.

CHRISTMAS BRUNCH
AT OLD CHURCH
MIMI MCMAKIN AND CELERIE KEMBLE

TO A CHILD, THE MAGIC OF CHRISTMAS knows no bounds. From the flash and spangle of glittering lights to fireside stories of Santa Claus and his elves, all is wondrous.

At the home of Leigh and Mimi Maddock McMakin, one of the oldest properties in Palm Beach, a similarly whimsical spirit fills the halls all year long. Here, giant silk butterflies hang from the ceiling and tasseled end-table parasols punctuate an expansive living room. Everything from oil paintings to the house manager's shorts hangs from the walls, and every surface is peppered with family photos, animal figurines, and children's toys.

The oft-photographed menagerie housed in the former Bethesda-by-the-Sea Episcopal Church building now known as Old Church mirrors the family's irreverent entertaining style: Anything goes. Dinner with the McMakins—almost always assembled on a moment's notice—might mean individual wine bottles strung from the ceiling over each place setting, pink rubber snakes in the salad, or plywood tables covered with palm fronds for oyster roasts along the bicycle trail in the backyard.

There is perhaps no more merry a gathering than on Christmas Day. "The house is already so magical that when you layer it with Christmas lights and tinsel and the foreshadowing of presents to suddenly appear, it is just humming with kid enthusiasm," interior designer Celerie Kemble says of her childhood home, built in 1894 and deconsecrated in 1925, when the congregation relocated to South County Road.

"I grew up next door," Mimi says of Tree Tops, one of the homes in the Maddock family compound. "And my father grew up one house to the north at Duck's Nest, where we had Christmas, so this has been going on for about 120 years between our families."

As the children clamor to the tree on Christmas morning, wrapping paper flies and squeals of joy fill the air. Adults emerge in bathrobes and pajamas for mimosas, coffee, and hot cocoa, nibbling on Nancy Murray's coffee cake (a family favorite) and plates of cheese, pâté, and cornichons.

Bring nature to the table. Use fresh plant material. It doesn't have to be flowers. We use big leaves as placemats. Natural objects are the most important; things we can find or cut ourselves. Our biggest shells (used to serve condiments) were found on the west coast of Florida on an island called Useppa.

Let guests help themselves to the bar. We'll make their first drink, and then everyone makes their own. We'll set a tray out with lots of glasses and different wines in buckets. I think people love that because they don't have to wait to be served again.

Keep it real. We're only interested in entertaining if what we're doing is actually fun, and that means keeping things as informal and natural as possible. It's not about showing how perfect you can get your house in one night. Then guests feel included and invited into something sacred or real.

Reinvent found objects as party decor. Find things that are distinctive that don't take a lot of adornment to look special, and keep a roving treasure chest of stuff you like. You can always reassemble it in different ways that are meaningful for different holidays or table settings.

Once sunlight has filtered through the storied stained-glass windows at Old Church, Celerie's sister, Phoebe Kemble, a classically trained chef, takes over in the kitchen while Mimi and Celerie set the table with holiday linens, treasured pieces from the family's John Maddock & Sons Thatched Cottage Ware dish collection, and hand-painted holiday glasses, a gift from Mimi's stepmother. Personalized birdhouse ornaments denote place settings, while a frog-trimmed tulipiere brought home from a trip to San Miguel de Allende, Mexico, serves as a centerpiece and conversation starter. Soon, a casual brunch buffet emerges with a bounty of chicken hash, crêpes, fresh fruit, and more for the myriad friends and family (Mimi has eight siblings) who will come and go all day through doors that always remain open. "It's more 'doors wide open' than 'table elaborately set,'" says Celerie of Christmases at home.

Celerie, husband Boykin Curry, and their three children never miss a Christmas at Old Church. At one, three, and four years old respectively, Wick, Zinnia, and Rascal represent the sixth generation to trim the family tree on Palm Beach. "Having such a chain of unbroken continuity means that I'm thinking less as a parent and more as a child, and I love being here, so I like to share with my children what still means so much to me," says Celerie.

CHICKEN HASH OVER WILD RICE, SERVED WITH CURRANT
JELLY

PHOEBE KEMBLE'S FAMOUS "CRAVE-IT" SALAD

POPOVERS WITH SIMPLY SCRUMPTIOUS
STRAWBERRY BUTTER

BINA'S CRÊPES WITH BLUEBERRIES AND SYRUP,
ORANGE MARMALADE,
CINNAMON APPLESAUCE, CARAMELIZED PINEAPPLE,
OR NUTELLA AND BANNANA

SELECTION OF TROPICAL FRUITS, INCLUDING MIMI'S
HOME-GROWN STAR FRUITS

HOT CHOCOLATE WITH HOMEMADE MARSHMALLOWS

CHICKEN HASH

For many of us hash is a dish filled with meat, potatoes, and spices served at breakfast. This old classic is a variation on the theme and best served as a brunch dish with wild rice and currant jelly. It is also delicious wrapped in a crêpe and topped with currant jelly or poured over crisp French bread.

Serves 8

1½	pounds boneless, skinless chicken breasts
	Salt and freshly ground black pepper
3	cups chicken broth, preferably low-sodium
½	cup (1 stick) unsalted butter
½	cup all-purpose flour
¼	cup dry fine sherry
¼	cup heavy cream
1½	pounds Gruyère cheese, grated
¼	teaspoon grated nutmeg
¼	teaspoon chili powder
¼	cup grated Parmesan cheese
¼	cup plain bread crumbs
	Wild rice and currant jelly for serving

Season the chicken breasts with salt and pepper.

In a large saucepan, bring the chicken broth to a boil over medium-high heat. Add the chicken and lower the heat to medium-low. Poach the chicken until cooked through, about 20 minutes. Remove the chicken from the broth and set aside to cool. Reserve the broth. When the chicken is cool enough to handle, cut it into 1-inch cubes.

Melt the butter in a separate large saucepan over low heat and add the flour. Stir with a whisk until totally combined. Add the broth, sherry, and heavy cream, a little at a time, and continue whisking to make a thick, smooth sauce. Add the Gruyère cheese, nutmeg, and chili powder and whisk until the cheese is melted. Remove from the heat and stir in the reserved chicken.

Preheat the oven to 500°F.

Transfer the chicken mixture to a decorative oven-to-table dish. In a small bowl, combine the Parmesan cheese and bread crumbs. Sprinkle the mixture on top of the hash, place in the broiler, and broil until the top is golden brown, about 5 minutes. Serve immediately, with wild rice and currant jelly.

Clockwise from top: Chicken Hash; Wild Rice; Tropical Fruits, and Currant Jelly

PHOEBE KEMBLE'S FAMOUS "CRAVE-IT" SALAD

This salad is the best when paired with our Christmas chicken hash, given its vibrant shades of green and bright lemony flavor. For another gathering, this salad can be made into a full one-stop meal by adding grilled chicken or shrimp. Be sure to chop all the vegetables and avocado into even, bite-size pieces.

Serves 8

½	cup extra-virgin olive oil
2	cups chopped asparagus
3	medium zucchini, chopped
	Salt
¼	cup fresh lemon juice
2	teaspoons balsamic vinegar
3	ripe avocados, peeled, pitted, and chopped
8	ounces arugula
	Small wedge of Parmesan cheese, shaved into bite-size pieces
	Freshly ground black pepper

Heat ¼ cup of the olive oil in a large sauté pan over medium heat. Add the asparagus and zucchini, season with salt, and sauté until cooked though but still firm, 7 to 10 minutes. Set aside to cool, then drain any excess liquid.

In a small bowl, whisk together the remaining ¼ cup olive oil, the lemon juice, ½ teaspoon salt, and the vinegar. Pour a few spoonfuls of the lemon dressing over the avocado to keep it from browning.

Combine the asparagus, zucchini, arugula, avocado, and cheese (reserving a little cheese for serving) in salad bowl and pour half of the dressing over the salad. Toss well and season with black pepper; add more dressing if needed, or set the remaining dressing on the table for guests to use. Sprinkle the salad with the remaining cheese before serving.

SIMPLY SCRUMPTIOUS STRAWBERRY BUTTER

There is no need to cook, hull, or strain berries with this easy recipe. The key is choosing a wonderful butter (we like Beurre d'Isigny) and a fabulous strawberry jam. Eric Bur makes superb jams, and we found some of our favorites at the local farmers' market. This is a recipe you can have fun with. Try fig, raspberry, or any jam you love and serve it in unexpected "dishes." Mimi chose to serve her jam in seashells, bringing nature to the table and adding a bit of whimsy to her lakeside Christmas buffet.

Makes 3 cups

2	cups (4 sticks) unsalted butter, softened
7	ounces strawberry jam

Put the butter in a blender and, adding the strawberry jam in batches, blend until smooth. Transfer to a decorative dish and serve immediately, or cover and refrigerate until ready to use. Take out of the refrigerator 10 minutes before serving to allow the butter to soften.

BINA'S CRÊPES

Crêpes originate from Brittany, a region in the northwest of France, where they are traditionally served with cider, but for this Christmas buffet Mimi and Celerie offer a variety of crowd-pleasing fillings and toppings.

Substituting the milk in this recipe with equal parts condensed and evaporated milk yields a thicker crêpe, perfect for making cheese blintzes. Swap out the vanilla extract for 1 teaspoon Cointreau and you have a more richly flavored crêpe, perfect for an evening dessert.

Makes 10 to 12 crêpes

1	cup all-purpose flour
2½	cups whole milk
3	large eggs
1	teaspoon salt
1	teaspoon grapeseed oil
⅛	teaspoon vanilla extract
2	tablespoons unsalted butter

In a blender, combine the flour and milk and blend until smooth. Add the eggs, salt, and oil and blend until smooth, then add the vanilla. Allow to rest for 30 minutes, or cover and refrigerate overnight.

Heat a 10-inch cast-iron skillet over high heat until very hot. Lower the heat to medium-high and add 1 tablespoon of the butter to the pan. Pour ⅓ cup batter into the bottom of the pan, pick up the pan, and tilt it in a circle so the batter covers the bottom of the pan. Cook until the edges of the crêpe start to lift from the pan, about 30 seconds. Use a spatula to lift the crêpe and flip it over in the pan. Cook for 15 seconds, then move to a warm decorative plate. Repeat with remaining batter, adding more butter to the pan as needed, and stacking the crêpes on a plate.

Guests can roll their crêpes around their favorite fillings or simply fold into quarters and cover with marmalade, applesauce, fruit, or strawberry butter.

CARAMELIZED PINEAPPLE

Mimi and Celerie served these flavorful rounds with homemade crêpes. For an evening meal, top them with coconut sorbet to create a tropical dessert. The pineapple will likely release juice as it cooks. Save this sweet, buttery sauce to drizzle over your crêpes, or if using the rings for an evening dessert, drizzle over sorbet or ice cream. They also make a great topping for cheesecake. Be sure to begin with a fresh ripe pineapple for the best results.

Makes 10 to 12 slices

2	tablespoons unsalted butter, melted
½	cup packed brown sugar
1	pineapple, cored and cut into ½-inch-thick pineapple rings

Preheat the broiler. Arrange the rack so it is 6 to 8 inches from the heat.

Pour the melted butter into a large broiler-proof cassserole dish and arrange the pineapple slices on the dish in a single layer. Crumble the brown sugar over the pineapple slices, being sure to cover each ring entirely. It is fine to allow some sugar to pool in the center of the ring.

Place the dish under the broiler and broil until the sugar melts and caramelizes and the pineapple is tender, about 5 minutes.

Remove the dish, flip the slices over, and return to the broiler for another 5 minutes, or until the pineapple browns slightly. Serve hot.

COASTAL COOL
TRACY AND MATT SMITH

TRACY SMITH'S SIGNATURE STYLE is evident in the beautiful pieces she hand selects for her vintage jewelry boutique, House of Lavande. While the objects themselves offer a sparkling window to the beauty of eras past, Tracy's vision is thoroughly modern—and that sums up her approach to every aspect of her lifestyle, from her wardrobe choices to the way she entertains.

As she sets the table for dinner at her oceanfront cabana, Tracy's personal style comes through in a studied combination of natural elements and glamorous metallic accents. She achieves that effect by layering, a technique she employs whether dressing herself or her table. A floor-length ikat tablecloth is topped with a coarse linen runner, on which are placed corals, sea fans, and barnacles in a palette of neutral tones with pops of lavender— her signature color. The elements impart a note of elegance while evoking the rhythm and flow of the coral reef below the ocean surface.

Hammered metal chargers sit beneath graphic Jacques Bernardaud plates, each with a different fish depicted against a modern grid pattern. For a vintage touch, she uses cut-crystal, gold-rimmed wine goblets, accompanied by simple water tumblers for a mixed-and-matched effect. Mercury glass votives and gilded vases add another touch of glimmer.

Tonight Tracy and Matt Smith are hosting a group of friends for a coastal-themed dinner by the sea. While she always insists on creating a chic, elegant ambiance, her sensibility as a wife and mother of two remains rooted in casual comforts.

"We like to keep it casual and fun," she says. "Matt loves to do the music selection and make up specialty drinks like the Dark and Stormy for parties."

Upon arrival, the Smiths' guests sip summer peach sangria, complete with frozen stirring cubes laced with lavender sprigs, thyme, and fresh berries, as Matt's mix of soulful tunes plays on. Bulb lights hang above the open-air terrace that sits just steps beyond the surf line, creating a softly lit Saint-Tropez-at-dusk mood. The lights also have a practical function: Since sea turtles nest on Palm Beach's shores during the spring months, exterior lights on beachfront properties have to be kept to a minimum.

Send unique invitations, even if you are hosting a small dinner—it makes it feel more special.

Have a specialty drink other than Champagne or wine to serve as guests arrive; it's a good conversation starter.

Prepare a terrific mix of music that speaks to your own personal listening style. It makes the evening feel more personal.

Don't be too preoccupied with timing, and don't stress about getting everyone seated.

As the evening progresses, the group of friends finds its way to the dinner table, which is glowing beneath the subtle lighting. The furnishings—sea grass garden stools in place of ballroom chairs, and a banquette layered in Provençal-inspired throw pillows—speak to casual comfort, inviting guests to relax through the three-course seafood feast.

A savory Provençal fish soup is served in fresh sea urchin shells flown in from the Mediterranean coast, while oyster shells cradle spicy scallops and ceviche. Chanterelle mushrooms and fava bean puree punch up fillets of Chilean sea bass, and summer citrus flavors infuse an orange granita—served with whoopie pies, another nod to the past—for dessert.

"My stepmother is very artistic and taught me to see the beauty in all my surroundings, not just traditional beauty," Tracy says. "And how, like a painting, when you piece together what you see as beautiful, it becomes a work of art in itself."

To that effect, Tracy is always sure to send special invitations for even the most casual of gatherings. "Even if it's a small dinner, it makes it feel more special," she says, noting the hand-calligraphed invitations, menus, and place cards procured for tonight's dinner. "I always assign seating prior with a handwritten or engraved card. It shows you took the time to consider who your guests' dinner partners would be." And dinnertime goes with the flow. "If the mood seems to call for more socializing before dinner, I don't stress about getting everyone seated."

It is perhaps the greatest example of the Palm Beach lifestyle as it was originally meant to be: effortless yet elegant, combining the riches of the globe with the comforts of home. And cocktails. Lots of cocktails.

MENU FOR EIGHT

SUMMER PEACH SANGRIA

ROASTED FENNEL AND ONION PIZZA

GUACAMOLE AND OLIVE TAPENADE

FISH SOUP PROVENÇAL

SPICY CEVICHE OF SEA SCALLOPS IN OYSTER SHELLS

SEARED SEA BASS OVER FAVA BEAN PUREE
WITH ASPARAGUS TIPS AND CHANTERELLE MUSHROOMS

ORANGE GRANITA

THE SUGAR MONKEY'S LEMON RASPBERRY WHOOPIE PIES

ROASTED FENNEL AND ONION PIZZA

This pizza is chic as an hors d'oeuvre, and we love it for more casual entertaining, too. Consider serving individual pizzas with a side salad and sangria for a more relaxed evening.

Serves 8 as an appetizer

6	tablespoons extra-virgin olive oil
2	small fennel bulbs, thinly sliced
1	large yellow onion, thinly sliced
2	tablespoons anise seeds
	Salt and freshly ground black pepper
¼	cup finely chopped fennel fronds
2	medium pizza dough balls, flattened according to the package instructions, or store-bought crusts
4	ounces burrata cheese, diced

Preheat the oven to 500°F.

Heat 4 tablespoons of the olive oil in a large sauté pan over medium heat. Add the fennel and onion slices and cook until the onions are golden brown and soft, 8 to 10 minutes. Add the anise seeds and season with salt and pepper. Stir in the fennel fronds.

Place the pizza doughs or crusts on a cookie sheet and drizzle each with 1 tablespoon of olive oil. Divide the onion-fennel mixture on each and spread, leaving a 1-inch border at the edges. Sprinkle the cheese on top and season with salt and pepper.

Place in the oven and bake for 10 minutes, or until the cheese is melted and the edges are golden brown. Slice into wedges or squares and serve hot.

Top left: Spicy Ceviche of Sea Scallops in Oyster Shells; Top right: Guacamole and Olive Tapenade; Bottom: Roasted Fennel and Onion Pizza

FISH SOUP PROVENÇAL

Presentation can elevate any dish to the magnificent. Tracy's sea urchin vessels wowed her guests, but serving this delicious soup in a beautiful bowl would be just as lovely.

Serves 8

4	tablespoons extra-virgin olive oil
1	large fennel bulb, sliced
1	leek (white and light green parts only), sliced
4	celery stalks, sliced
1	large yellow onion, sliced
3	cloves garlic, sliced
	Salt and freshly ground black pepper
1	cup white wine
1	large tomato, diced
8	cups vegetable stock, preferably low-sodium and homemade
1	tablespoon saffron threads
16	large shrimp, peeled
8	large scallops
8	medium mussels, cleaned
8	medium or small clams, cleaned
¼	cup finely chopped fresh flat-leaf parsley

In a large saucepan, heat 3 tablespoons of the olive oil over medium heat. Add the fennel, leek, celery, onion, and garlic and sauté until the onion is just translucent, 5 to 7 minutes. Season with salt and pepper. Add the wine, bring to a boil, and cook until the wine is reduced by half. Add the tomatoes and cook until softened, about 15 minutes. Add the vegetable stock and saffron, crushing the saffron with your fingers as it goes into the pan. Bring to a simmer.

Meanwhile, heat the remaining 1 tablespoon of olive oil in a separate large saucepan. Add the shrimp and scallops and cook until just opaque, about 4 minutes (they will continue to cook in the soup). Add to the vegetable mixture. Add the mussels and clams to the mixture and cook until they open, about 6 minutes. Discard any mussles or clams that do not open. Serve immediately.

ORANGE GRANITA

This icy dessert is perfect for summer nights by the sea.

Serves 8

1	(12-ounce) can orange juice concentrate
1	cup sugar
1	cup fresh orange juice (about 6 oranges)
2	tablespoons fresh lemon juice

Dissolve the orange juice concentrate with the sugar in a sauté pan over low heat. Remove from the heat and cool to room temperature. Add the fresh orange and lemon juices and pour into a shallow freezer-proof dish.

Place in the freezer for 1 hour. Using a fork, flake the granita. Return to the freezer for another hour and flake again. Repeat until the desired texture is achieved, about 3 hours in total.

To serve, scrape the granita into a decorative glass or sorbet dish. Smith serves hers with a whoopie pie (page 200) on the side.

THE SUGAR MONKEY'S LEMON RASPBERRY WHOOPIE PIES

Makes 8 pies

1¾	cups all-purpose flour
¼	teaspoon baking powder
¼	teaspoon baking soda
¼	cup whole milk, at room temperature
4	tablespoons fresh orange juice, at room temperature
1	teaspoon white vinegar
4	tablespoons (½ stick) unsalted butter, at room temperature
1½	cups granulated sugar
½	teaspoon salt
	Zest of 1 lemon
2	large whole eggs, at room temperature
1	pint fresh raspberries
4	large egg whites, at room temperature
½	cup (1 stick) unsalted butter, cut into tablespoons, at room temperature
1	cup confectioners' sugar, sifted
1	tablespoon fresh lemon juice

Preheat the oven to 350°F.

Sift the flour, baking powder, and baking soda into a large bowl.

Combine the milk, 2 tablespoons of the orange juice, and the vinegar in a small bowl.

In the bowl of an electric mixer fitted with the paddle attachment, cream the 4 tablespoons of butter, 1 cup of the granulated sugar, the salt, and lemon zest until light and fluffy. Add the whole eggs, one at a time, scraping the bowl between additions. Mix until combined.

With the mixer on low speed, add the flour mixture alternating with the milk mixture in 3 additions, scraping the bowl after each addition before adding the next. After the last of the milk mixture has been added, scrape the sides and bottom of the bowl and mix on medium speed for 2 minutes to incorporate all of the ingredients.

Scoop the mixture into greased muffin pans, 2 tablespoons per hole, to fill 16 holes. Place in the oven and bake for 15 minutes, or until golden brown. Turn out onto a rack to cool.

To make the raspberry buttercream, puree the raspberries in a blender and strain the seeds through a fine-mesh sieve.

Bring a medium saucepan of water over medium heat and bring to a simmer. Beat the egg whites and the remaining ½ cup granulated sugar in a heavy-bottomed metal bowl and place on the pan of simmering water on the stovetop. Beat until the temperature of the mixture reaches 104°F on an instant-read thermometer. Transfer the mixture to an electric mixer fitted with the whisk attachment and beat on medium-high speed until fluffy and cooled. Turn the speed down to medium and begin adding the softened butter by the tablespoon, beating well after each addition. Turn the mixer to low and slowly add the pureed raspberries; mix until incorporated. Set aside at room temperature.

To make the lemon icing, beat the confectioners' sugar, lemon juice, and the remaining 2 tablespoons of orange juice in a small bowl. If the icing is too thick, add some more juice to reach your desired consistency.

To assemble the whoopie pies, lay out half of the lemon cake halves and top with the raspberry buttercream using either a spoon or a pastry bag fitted with a plain tip. Top the remaining lemon cake halves with the lemon icing and place on top of the raspberry buttercream. Any extra cream and lemon icing may be refrigerated in an airtight container for up to 1 week.

The whoopie pies may be wrapped in plastic wrap and stored in the refrigerator for 3 days; bring to room temperature before serving.

IN GOOD TASTE
MORE RECIPES FROM FRIENDS

are known for celebrations as glittering and elaborate as the dresses they design. They love to mix and match, introduce surprising elements, and wow their guests with romantic, super-embellished tables and over-the-top displays. Badgley sets the scene as Mischka does his magic in the kitchen. The duo shares recipes for classic hors d'oeuvres and cocktails for a vintage Hollywood-themed party.

COLD TOMATO SOUP

This quick and easy recipe is based on an all-time favorite of actor Jack Lemmon. Add delightful elegance by serving it in vintage glasses or decorative shot glasses.

Serves 12

3	pounds ripe tomatoes, peeled and quartered
2	lemons, juiced
2	tablespoons lemon peel, grated
1	teaspoon granulated sugar
1	teaspoon salt
½	teaspoon ground pepper
1	bunch fresh chives for garnish

In a blender, puree the tomatoes with the lemon juice. Add the lemon peel, sugar, salt, and pepper. Strain through a fine sieve to remove tomato seeds. Chill in the refrigerator for at least two hours. Serve very cold. Pour into decorative glasses and garnish with whole chives.

MOSCOW MULE

This 1940s cocktail was wildly popular in Los Angeles in the mid-twentieth century. Use a good-quality ginger beer.

Makes 1 drink

½	lime, juiced
2	ounces vodka
8	ounces ginger beer
	Lime slices to garnish

Pour lime juice into a chilled mug or iced glass. Add vodka, then top off with ginger beer and decorate with a slice of lime.

GRAVLAKS

Be sure to begin with fresh salmon and leave the skin on as it adds flavor and makes carving easier. We love serving this cured salmon in a variety of ways: as an elegant appetizer; as an hors d'oeuvre on toast points with a mustard dill sauce, capers, and dill; or served Norwegian style as an open-faced sandwich.

Serves 24

3	tablespoons salt
3	tablespoons sugar
1	tablespoon crushed peppercorns
½	teaspoon dill seeds
1	(2 pound) salmon fillet, with skin
½	bunch fresh dill, coarsely chopped

Mix salt, sugar, peppercorns, and dill seeds together. Cut salmon in half lengthwise. Remove any pin bones. Place one half of fillet, skin-side down, in a baking dish. Sprinkle with half of the salt, sugar, peppercorn, and dill seed mixture. Then, cover with fresh dill. Rub the other half of the salmon with the remaining mixture and lay this piece over the other, skin side up. Wrap well in foil or plastic. Place a weighted plate on top of fish. Refrigerate for 48 hours, turning fish every 12 hours. Each time, unwrap and baste fillets with pan liquid and rewrap well. The gravlax is ready when the flesh is opaque. When ready to serve, carefully scrape off dill and seasonings. Place the fish skin side down on a cutting board and slice very thinly on the diagonal, cutting away from the skin.

CLUB COLETTE'S
"MRS. PANNILL'S BISCUITS"

Dan Ponton, owner of Club Colette, fondly recalls sitting at "table 15" and talking to Kit Pannill (see Gathering at the Lake House, page 18) at length about how to make Mrs. Walter "Barton" Gubelmann's birthday party special. Barton was a treasured friend and one of the first members Dan ever served at Club Colette. He asked Kit what signature recipes from her home would be the best possible dinner items, and when discussing bread, they thought biscuits would be clever. Mrs. Pannill's biscuits became the rage, and to this day they are the most requested bread item at the club.

Makes 20 biscuits

2½	cups self-rising flour, preferably White Lily, plus more for the work surface
½	cup heavy cream
3	tablespoons unsalted butter, melted

Preheat the oven to 400°F.

In a large bowl, mix the flour with the heavy cream to make a sticky dough. Place on a lightly floured surface and lightly flour the top of the dough. Pat or roll it out to a ½-inch thickness. Use a 2-inch cookie cutter to cut the biscuits in an "up and down" motion, never twisting, to make them rise.

Place the biscuits on an ungreased baking sheet and bake until golden brown, 8 to 10 minutes. Brush with melted butter and serve immediately.

NANCY CARTER'S
RAW CHOCOLATE TRUFFLES

Nancy Carter, one of Palm Beach's most remarkable hostesses, became hooked on the raw food lifestyle after tasting a "green drink" after a yoga class. "It made me feel like my skin came alive," she recalls. Eating raw, she says, makes her feel healthy, vibrant, and sated. She especially loves raw desserts, which are wholesome and healthful. Her chocolate truffles are a good example. They are free of animal products, refined sugars, and empty calories. Besides, she says, "They are so pretty to serve, and I've often made platefuls for friends."

Makes 25 to 27 truffles

1	cup raw cashew butter
¼	cup coconut oil or coconut butter
2	tablespoons raw agave nectar
2	tablespoons maple syrup
	Pinch of pink Himalayan salt
3	heaping tablespoons raw cacao powder
¼	cup your choice of toppings: raw coconut flakes, raw cacao powder, chopped pecans or walnuts, crushed dehydrated nuts

Place all the ingredients (it's best if they are at room temperature) except the toppings in a food processor and process until smooth. Transfer to a container, cover, and refrigerate until cold, about ½ hour.

Using a small melon-baller, scoop out the mixture, forming it into bite-size balls. Finish with the topping of your choice and serve. The truffles will keep refrigerated in an airtight container for up to 2 days.

EMILIA FANJUL'S CHICKEN SCALLOPS WITH MUSTARD SAUCE

"This is a great everyday dish and sensational for family entertaining," says Emilia, one of the savviest hostesses in Palm Beach and New York City. Everyone from toddlers to the pickiest of adults will love this dish. Serve it with buttered noodles or a fluffy white rice to absorb all that delicious sauce.

Serves 4

8	chicken breast cutlets, pounded thin
1/3	cup all-purpose flour
	Salt and freshly ground black pepper
4	tablespoons (½ stick) unsalted butter
2	tablespoons thinly sliced shallots
¼	cup white wine
½	cup heavy cream
1	tablespoon Dijon-style or Dusseldorf mustard

Place the chicken cutlets on a flat surface and, using a meat mallet, pound them until thin.

In a shallow bowl, season the flour with salt and pepper and dredge the cutlets on both sides, shaking off excess.

In a large skillet over medium heat, melt the butter until melted but not browned. Working in batches, cook the chicken on both sides until golden brown, 5 minutes per side. Transfer to a serving plate and cover with aluminum foil to keep warm.

To the same pan, add the shallots and cook until softened, about 4 minutes, then add the wine and cook until totally evaporated. Add the heavy cream, bring to a boil, then turn off the heat. Whisk in the mustard and spoon over the chicken cutlets. Serve immediately.

EVELYN LAUDER'S AVOCADO-HERB SALAD

Evelyn Lauder was a consummate Palm Beach hostess, and quite a good cook. Here on the island, she was particularly known for her salads with citrus and avocados picked from the trees at her oceanfront home. When the avocados were ripe and plentiful, she was inspired to host a party and serve light, local dishes like this salad. Fresh avocados can be paired with any Florida fruit to create a tasty and healthful salad, and Evelyn often varied up the recipe by using tangerines, oranges, and even papaya.

Serves 4

FOR THE DRESSING

2	tablespoons avocado oil or extra-virgin olive oil
	Juice of 2 limes
	Salt and freshly ground black pepper

FOR THE SALAD

2	ripe but firm avocados
2	limes, peeled and cut into segments
1	cup fresh basil leaves
½	cup fresh mint leaves
1	tablespoon minced fresh tarragon
1	Belgian endive, leaves separated

In a small bowl, whisk together the oil and lime juice. Season with salt and pepper.

Halve, pit, and peel the avocados. Slice them lengthwise and arrange on a serving dish with the lime segments, basil, mint, tarragon, and endive. Drizzle with the dressing and serve.

PAELLA RICA FROM THE KITCHEN AT VILLA YAS

Always flavorful and delicious, this paella is a family favorite of the owners of Villa Yas, a private home. You can use Vigo Yellow rice, a yellow rice with saffron, but we prefer long-grain rice, saffron, and a touch of turmeric to impart a rich, custard-like yellow color. It is best to use a 16-inch paella pan with lid to be sure it will fit in the oven, but a large sauté pan can work just as well.

Serves 8

8	chicken thighs
	Salt and freshly ground black pepper
½	cup extra-virgin olive oil
1	cup diced onion
1	cup julienned red bell pepper
1	cup julienned green bell pepper
12	ounces chorizo or chicken sausage, sliced
8	tablespoons finely chopped garlic
3	cups long-grain rice or Arborio rice
½	teaspoon ground turmeric
6	cups chicken stock, plus more if needed, preferably low-sodium
	Pinch of saffron
4	lobster tails in the shell, split
24	shrimp, peeled and deveined
24	clams
24	mussels

Preheat the oven to 350°F.

Season the chicken with salt and pepper.

Cover the bottom of a paella pan with the olive oil, heat over medium heat, and bring the oil to the smoke point. Add the chicken and cook on both sides until halfway cooked through, about 8 minutes. Remove the chicken from the pan. Add the onions, peppers, and chorizo, and sauté for 5 minutes, or until the onions are translucent.

Add 4 tablespoons of the garlic, the rice, and turmeric to the pan and season with salt and pepper; mix well to combine all the ingredients. Remove the skin and bones from the chicken thighs (or you may leave them in if you prefer). Arrange the chicken thighs so they are spread evenly around the outside of the pan.

Warm the chicken stock in a medium saucepan until hot. Crumble in the saffron and pour 5 cups of the stock over the rice mixture. The broth should be approximately ¼ inch above the rice. Add more broth or lower the heat and reduce the liquid if necessary.

Cover the pan tightly, place in the oven, and bake for 15 to 20 minutes, until the broth is reduced and nearly totally evaporated and the rice has begun cooking but remains moist.

Rub the remaining 4 tablespoons garlic inside the lobster tails and on the shrimp.

Remove the pan from the oven and evenly arrange the lobster, clams, and mussels over the top. Pour ¾ cup of the remaining stock over the mixture, cover tightly, and return to the oven for 10 to 15 minutes, checking that the rice is not getting overcooked or dry.

Add the shrimp and the remaining ¼ cup stock, return to the oven again, and bake for an additional 5 to 10 minutes, until the shellfish is completely cooked and the clams and mussels are open. Discard any clams or mussels that do not open.

Remove from the oven and gently arrange the shellfish to make the best presentation. Serve immediately directly from the pan.

PIPER QUINN'S MANGO-CHIPOTLE BRAISED PORK TACOS

Palm Beach resident and entrepreneur, Oliver "Piper" Quinn has much invested in the island, both personally and professionally. As a restaurateur, this man about town opened the wildly successful būccan, and brought a fresh, new food-centric energy to the dining scene in Palm Beach. His childhood home is featured in An Offering of Love, page 86.

Serves 6

3	large ripe mangoes, peeled and diced
1	(7-ounce) can chipotle chiles in adobo
¼	cup honey
½	cup soy sauce, preferably low-sodium
2	cloves garlic, chopped
½	cup fresh lime juice
	Salt
1	(5- to 6-pound) bone-in pork shoulder (Boston butt)
24	flour tortillas, warmed
	Piper Quinn's Slaw (recipe follows) for serving
	Salsa for serving

Preheat the oven to 300°F.

In a blender, combine the mangoes, chipotles and sauce, honey, soy sauce, garlic, and lime juice.

Put the pork, fat side up, in a deep-bottomed roasting pan. Pour the chipotle sauce on top, cover tightly with a lid or aluminum foil, and bake for 2 hours. Turn and bake for another 2 hours, or until the meat easily falls off the bone.

Transfer the meat to a cutting board and set aside until it is cool enough to handle. Using 2 forks, shred the meat.

Transfer the sauce to a saucepan, skimming as much fat as possible. Warm the sauce, season with salt and pepper, and add to the pulled pork.

To serve, arrange the pulled pork on a platter and serve with warm tortillas, slaw, and salsa.

PIPER QUINN'S SLAW

3	cups sliced Napa cabbage
3	medium carrots, julienned
2	tablespoons chopped fresh cilantro
1	large green apple, peeled, cored, and julienned
½	cup cider vinegar
½	cup orange juice
3	tablespoons extra-virgin olive oil
1	tablespoon honey
	Salt

In a large bowl, toss together the cabbage, carrots, cilantro, and apple.

In a small bowl, whisk together the vinegar, orange juice, olive oil, and honey; season with salt. Pour the dressing over the cabbage mixture and toss to combine. Cover and refrigerate until ready to serve. The slaw can be prepared a day ahead.

SUE AND JAMES PATTERSON'S GRANDMA'S KILLER CHOCOLATE CAKE

This recipe, which was handed down by Sue Patterson's grandmother, is a staple at Patterson family gatherings and special occasions. Every year Sue bakes the cake for James's and her mother's birthdays, which are two days apart. "We put it on a glass cake stand—a gift from Jim's sister because we made the cake so often—and after the singing, candle blowing, and the initial serving, it mysteriously disappears," Sue says. Use the best chocolate you can find, as the flavor will affect the outcome. You can substitute organic whole-wheat flour to give the cake a stronger depth of flavor and a wonderful wholesomeness.

Makes 1 (9-inch) cake; serves 10

FOR THE CAKE

½	cup (1 stick) unsalted butter
7	ounces semisweet chocolate, chopped
⅔	cup unsalted butter, at room temperature
2	cups sugar
2	large eggs
2	cups all-purpose flour
1⅓	cups buttermilk
1⅓	teaspoons baking soda, dissolved in ½ cup warm water
1	teaspoon vanilla extract

FOR THE CHOCOLATE GANACHE

½	cup (1 stick) unsalted butter
6	ounces semisweet chocolate, chopped
2	cups sugar
⅔	cup milk
1	teaspoon vanilla extract
1	teaspoon almond extract

Make the cake: Preheat the oven to 350°F and butter a 9-inch springform pan.

In a double boiler over very low heat, melt the chocolate, stirring until smooth. Remove from the heat and cool.

In the bowl of an electric mixer, cream the butter with the sugar until fluffy. Add the eggs, one at a time, mixing well between each addition. Add 1 cup of flour and the buttermilk and mix well. Add the remaining cup of flour and mix well. Stir in the dissolved baking soda, the melted chocolate, and the vanilla.

Pour the mixture into the prepared pan, place in the oven, and bake for about 40 minutes, until a skewer inserted in the center comes out dry. Place the pan on a wire rack to partially cool. When it is cool enough to handle, remove the sides of the pan.

Make the ganache: In a medium saucepan, melt the butter with the chocolate, sugar, milk, and vanilla and almond extracts over medium heat. Bring to a simmer, whisking until smooth; simmer for a minute to thicken. Remove from the heat and cool.

Assemble the cake: When the cake is cooled completely, use a long serrated knife to slice the cake into three horizontal pieces. Spread one third of the frosting between each layer. To finish, pour the remaining frosting on top and let it dribble down the sides. Slice and serve.

HOST SELECTIONS

CATERING

Blue Provence
300 South County Road
Palm Beach, FL 33480
(561) 651-1491
www.blueprovence.com

Christafaro's Catering
1200 Clare Avenue
West Palm Beach, FL 33401
(561) 835-0066
www.christafaroswpb.com

Christina's Catering
P.O. Box 2502
Palm Beach, FL 33480
(561) 261-7228
www.cateringpb.com

Christopher's Kitchen
4783 PGA Boulevard
Palm Beach Gardens, FL 33418
(561) 318-6191
www.christopherskitchenfl.com

Ken-Rose Catering & Event Planning
4188 Westroads Drive, Suites 108/109
West Palm Beach, FL 33407
(561) 882-0135
www.ken-rose.com

Ovations! Catering & Events
700 South Rosemary Avenue
West Palm Beach, FL 33409
(561) 308-1188
www.Ovations-catering.com

Palm Beach Catering
1109 25th Street, Suite A
West Palm Beach, FL 33407
(561) 833-1411
www.palmbeachcatering.com
Info@PalmBeachCatering.com

The White Apron
1710 N. Dixie Highway
Lake Worth, FL 33460
(561) 585-2985
www.whiteapron.org

EVENT PLANNERS

Beth Beattie Branding, PR and Events
Beth Beattie
214 Brazilian Avenue, Suite 200
Palm Beach, FL 33480
(561) 628-3058
www.bethbeattie.com

Elegant Affairs
Florence Seiler
(561) 758-3261

It! Weddings & Events
Aime Dunstan
P.O. Box 2183
Palm Beach, FL 33480
(561) 801-0767
www.itweddingsandevents.com

Ober, Onet & Associates
Polly Onet
Nine East 97th Street, No. 2D
New York, NY 10029
(561) 835-3501 Palm Beach
(212) 876-6775 New York
(631) 283-1141 Southampton
www.oberonet.com

Posh Parties & Paper
Heather Lowenthal
(561) 302-0702
www.poshpartiesonline.com

Rafanelli Events
Bryan Rafanelli
867 Boylston Street, 4th Floor
Boston, MA 02116
(617) 357-1818
www.rafanellievents.com

Sutra International Design Inc.
Bruce Sutka
424 Palm Street
West Palm Beach, FL 33401
(561) 835-8455
www.sutrainternationaldesign.com

Van Wyck & Van Wyck
Bronson Van Wyck
224 West 30th Street
New York, New York 10001
212-675-8601
www.vanwyck.net

FOR THE TABLE

Anthropologie
700 South Rosemary Avenue
West Palm Beach, FL 33401
(561) 805-8770
www.anthropologie.com

Asprey Miami
The Setai South Beach
2001 Collins Avenue
Miami Beach, FL 33139
(305) 532-2990
www.asprey.com

Asprey New York
853 Madison Avenue
New York, NY 10021
(212) 688-1811
www.asprey.com

Baccarat
625 Madison Avenue at 59th Street
New York, NY 10022
(212) 826-4100
www.baccarat.com

Barneys
660 Madison Avenue
New York, NY 10065
(212) 826-8900
www.barneys.com

Beach House
30 Main Street
Vineyard Haven, MA 02568
(508) 693-6091
www.thebeachhouse.com

Bergdorf Goodman
Fifth Avenue at 58th Street
New York, NY 10019
(800) 558-1855
www.bergdorfgoodman.com

Bliss Monogramming
111 East Boca Raton Road
Boca Raton, FL 33432
(561) 395-7048
www.blissdesignsinc.com

Bridge Kitchenware
17 Waverly Place
Madison, NJ 07940
(973) 377-3900
www.bridgekitchenware.com

Buccellati
46 East 57th Street
New York, NY 10022
(212) 308-2900
www.buccellati.com

Cartier
6000 Glades Road, Suite 1069
Boca Raton, FL
(561) 367-9100
www.cartier.com

Devonia Antiques
3703 South Dixie Highway
West Palm Beach, FL 33405
(561) 429-8566
www.devonia-antiques.com

Fabienne Marumo
302 South County Road
Palm Beach, FL 33480
(561) 296-5582

1stdibs@NYDC
200 Lexington Avenue, 10th
Floor
New York, NY 10016
(646) 293-6633
www.1stdibs.com

Fishs Eddy
889 Broadway
New York, NY 10003
(877) 347-4733
www.fishseddy.com

Frette
799 Madison Avenue
New York, NY 10021

(212) 988-5221
www.frette.com

FS Henemader Antiques
316 South County Road
Palm Beach, FL 33480
(561) 835-9237
www.fshenemaderantiques.com

Georg Jensen
230 North Rodeo Drive
Beverly Hills, CA 90210
(310) 860-1410
www.georgjensen.com

Hildreth's Home Goods
51-55 Main Street
Southampton, NY 11968
(631) 283-2300
www.hildreths.com

Home, James!
55 Main Street
East Hampton, NY 11937
(631) 324-2307
www.homejameseasthampton.com

Idlewild Furnishing
13501 South Shore Boulevard,
Suite 102
Wellington, FL 33414
(561) 793-1970
www.idlewildstables.com

Island Home Palm Beach
249 Royal Poinciana Way
Palm Beach, FL 33480
(561) 832-6244
www.islandhomepalmbeach.com

Kassatly's Palm Beach
250 Worth Avenue
Palm Beach, FL 33480
(561) 655-5655

Kim Seybert
(212) 564-7850
www.kimseybert.com

Kofski's Antiques
315 South County Road
Palm Beach, FL 33480
(561) 655-6557
www.kofski.com

Leta Austin Foster
64 Via Mizner
Palm Beach, FL 33480
(561) 655-7367
www.letaaustinfoster.com

Limoges France
41 Lake Drive
Mountain Lakes, NJ 07046
(973) 515-0824
www.limoges.com

**Lori Jayne Monogramming
& More**
305 South County Road
Palm Beach, FL 33480
(561) 514-9199

Mac Fabrics
428 Clematis Street
West Palm Beach, FL 33401
(561) 833-7000
www.macfabrics.com

MacKenzie-Childs
238 Worth Avenue
Palm Beach, FL 33480
(561) 832-9877
www.mackenzie-childs.com

Mallett Antiques
929 Madison Avenue
New York, NY 10021
(212) 249-8783
www.mallettantiques.com

Mary Mahoney
336 Worth Avenue
Palm Beach, FL 33480
(561) 655-8288
www.marymahoney.com

Mecox Gardens
3900 South Dixie Highway
West Palm Beach, FL 33405
(561) 805-8611
www.mecoxgardens.com

Neiman Marcus
151 Worth Avenue
Palm Beach, FL 33480
(561) 805-6150
www.neimanmarcus.com

Objects in the Loft
3611 South Dixie Highway
West Palm Beach, FL 33405
(561) 659-0403
www.objectsintheloft.com

Old Town Crossing
46 Main Street
Southampton, NY 11968
(631) 283-7740
www.oldtowncrossing.com

Pavillon Christofle
150 Worth Avenue
Palm Beach, FL 33480
(561) 833-1978

9700 Collins Avenue
Bal Harbour, FL 33154
(305) 864-0330
www.christofle.com

Pierre Frey
351 Peachtree Hills Avenue NE,
Suite 128
Atlanta, GA 30305
(404) 237-5079
www.pierrefrey.com

Pier One Imports
11275 Legacy Avenue
Palm Beach Gardens, FL 33410
(561) 624-5785
www.pier1.com

Pioneer Linens
210 Clematis Street
West Palm Beach, FL 33401
(800) 207-LINENS
www.pioneerlinens.com

Portobello Road
4 Dock Street
Edgartown, MA 02539
(508) 627-4276

Rainy Day
66 Main Street
Vineyard Haven, MA 02568
(508) 693-1830
www.rainydaymv.com

Ralph Lauren
501 East Cooper Avenue
Aspen, CO 81611
(970) 925-5147
www.ralphlauren.com

Restoration Hardware
700 South Rosemary Avenue,
Suite 112
West Palm Beach, FL 33401
(561) 804-6826
www.restorationhardware.com

Sara Lerner Ceramics
Available at Parasutra
 340 Royal Poinciana Way,
Suite 332B
Palm Beach, Fl 33480
And by appointment
(561) 385-0610
www.saralernerceramics.com

Scully & Scully
504 Park Avenue
New York, NY 10022
(800) 223-3717
www.scullyandscully.com

Simon Pearce
500 Park Avenue
New York, NY 10022
(212) 421-8801
www.simonpearce.com

Thomas Goode
19 South Audley Street
Mayfair, London
44 (0) 207 499 2823
www.thomasgoode.com

Tiffany & Co.
259 Worth Avenue
Palm Beach, FL 33480
(561) 659-6090
www.tiffany.com

Timeless Treasures
26 Main Street
Vineyard Haven, MA 02568
(508) 696-7637

T is for Table
4600 PGA Boulevard, Suite 105

Palm Beach Gardens, FL 33418
(561) 799-9733
www.tisfortable.com

Trousseau Fine Vintage Linen
219 Royal Poinciana Way, Suite 1
Palm Beach, FL 33480
(561) 832-9696

Extra Touch Flowers
420 Clematis Street
West Palm Beach, FL 33401
(561) 835-8000
www.extratouchflowers.com

Madison Floral
63B Inner Belt Road
Somerville, MA 02143
(617) 625-7500
www.madisonfloral.com

Perriwater Limited
960 First Avenue
New York, NY 10022
(212) 759-9313

Renny & Reed
505 Park Avenue
New York, NY 10022
(212) 288-7000
www.rennyandreed.com

The Special Event Resource
Michael Ereshena
1715 Old Okeechobee Road
West Palm Beach, FL 33409
(561) 686-7757
www.specialeventresource.com

Sweet Arrangements
139 North County Road,
Suite 10
Palm Beach, FL 33480
(561) 514-9791

Tom Mathieu & Co.
312 D Worth Avenue
Palm Beach, FL 33480
(561) 833-2179
www.tommathieu.com

Touch of Paradise Events
210 South E Street
Lake Worth, FL 33460
(561) 585-0580
www.touchofparadiseevents.com

VM Flowers
1600 Mercer Avenue, Suite 8
West Palm Beach, FL 33401
(561) 659-1466

William NYC Flowers
(347) 806-3851
william@williamnycflowers.com
www.williamnycflowers.com

Winston Flowers
131 Newbury Street
Boston, MA 02116
(800) 457-4901
www.winstonflowers.com

PARTY RENTALS
Atlas Party Rentals
131 Commerce Road
Boynton Beach, FL 33426
(561) 547-6565
www.atlaspartyrental.com

Big Sky Tent & Party Rentals
15 East Line Road
Edgartown MA 02539
(508) 693-2237
info@bigskytent.com
www.bigskytent.com

Bubble Miami
19400 West Dixie Highway
Aventura, FL 33180
(305) 761-6392
www.bubblemiami.com

Classic Party Rentals
41 Willow Road

Water Mill, NY 11976
(631) 726-6664
www.classicpartyrentals.com

Panache: A Classic Party Rentals Company
2744 Hillsboro Road
West Palm Beach, FL 33405
(561) 833-2188
www.linenswithpanache.com

Seaside Celebrations Tent & Party Rental
P.O. Box 2775
Vineyard Haven, MA 02568
(508) 693-0556
www.seasidecelebrations.com

Tentlogix
2820 SE Martin Square
Corporate Parkway
Stuart, FL 34994
(888) 34-PARTY
www.tentlogix.com

Tilton Tents and Party Rentals
147 Edgartown
Vineyard Haven Road
Vineyard Haven, MA 02568
Martha's Vineyard
www.tiltontents.com

SPECIALTY FOODS
Buttercup Bake Shop
973 Second Avenue
New York, NY 10022
(212) 350-4144
www.buttercupbakeshop.com

Cilantro's Gourmet Deli
3975 Isles View Drive
Wellington, FL 33414
(561) 296-6500

Citarella
2 Pantigo Road
Easthampton, NY 11937
(631) 537-5990
www.citarella.com

D'Artagnan
280 Wilson Avenue
Newark, NJ 07105
(800) 327-8246
www.dartagnan.com

El Bodegón
4481 Lake Worth Road
Lake Worth, FL 33461
(561) 967-2177

Farmhouse Tomatoes
Palm Beach County, FL
(561) 968-6971
www.farmhousetomatoes.com

4th Generation Organic Market
75 SE Third Street
Boca Raton, FL 33431
(561) 338-9920
www.4thgenerationmarket.com

Glaser Organic Farms
19100 SW 137 Avenue
Miami, FL 33177
(305) 238-7747
www.glaserorganicfarms.com

Global Organics
339 Massachusetts Avenue
Arlington, MA 02474
(781) 648-8844
www.global-organics.com

Maison Ladurée
864 Madison Avenue
New York, NY 10021
(646) 558-3157
www.laduree.fr

Pierre Hermé
72 rue Bonaparte 75006
Paris, France
01 43 54 47 77
www.pierreherme.com

Ristorante Sant Ambroeus
30 Main Street
Southampton, NY 11968
(631) 283-1233
www.santambroeus.com

Sugar Chef
2875 Sout Congress Avenue
Delray Beach, FL 33445
(954) 971-CAKE
www.sugarchef.com

The Sugar Monkey
5640 Corporate Way
West Palm Beach, FL 33407
(561) 689-7844
www.thesugarmonkey.com

Swank Specialty Produce
14311 North Road
Loxahatchee, FL 33470
(561) 202-5648
www.swankspecialtyproduce.
com

Tate's Bake Shoppe
43 North Sea Road
Southampton, NY 11968
(631) 283-9830
www.tatesbakeshop.com

Teuscher Chocolates of Switzerland
25 East 61st Street
New York, NY 10021
(800) 554-0624
www.teuscher.com

William Greenberg Desserts
1100 Madison Avenue
New York, NY 10028
(212) 861-1340
www.wmgreenbergdesserts.
com

STATIONERY AND GRAPHIC DESIGN

Alice B. King Fine Stationery
2454 Main Street
Bridgehampton, NY 11932
(631) 537-5115
www.alicebking.com

Barbara Brandt Calligraphy
alphabrandt@yahoo.com
(954) 971-0431

The Love List
Jessica@thelovelist.net
(805) 524-3894
www.thelovelist.net

The Printery
43 West Main Street
Oyster Bay, NY 11771
(516) 922-3250
www.iprintery.com

Signature Collection Inc.
505 S. Flagler Drive, Suite 404
West Palm Beach, FL 33401
(561) 655-1182
www.signaturecollection.com

Stationer on Sunrise
247 Sunrise Avenue
Palm Beach, FL 33480
(561) 833-7971
www.stationeronsunrise.com

Swoozie's
11701 Lake Victoria Gardens,
Suite 4104

Palm Beach Gardens, FL 33410
(561) 627-3744
www.swoozies.com

Truffie's of Palm Beach
350 South County Road,
Suite 102
Palm Beach, FL 33480
(561) 659-2284
www.palmbeachcatalog.com/
truffies.htm

Vivi's of Palm Beach
3 Via Parigi
Palm Beach, FL 33480
(561) 655-9374
www.vivispalmbeach.com

Vogel Bindery
30 Blue Jay Way
East Hampton, NY 11937
 (631) 329-3106
www.vogelbindery.com
Mail@vogelbindery.com

INDEX

ACKNOWLEDGMENTS

Creating this book has truly been a labor of love for me, but it has not been a solitary undertaking. When seeking to highlight the great work of CHS I would never have thought to produce this book without the encouragement of my dear friend Ellen Wright, and I would not have committed to tackle such a project without the support of Nasser and Yvonne Kazeminy, the greatest friends one could hope for.

I found the courage to begin this project when my coauthors and dear friends, Victoria Amory, Aime Dunstan, and Daphne Nikolopoulos, agreed to help. Collectively, they are the pure essence of this extraordinary project and the driving force behind its completion. They have each given generously of their time, energy, and talent, and have volunteered countless hours to ensure all elements of this book accurately reflect the grace and generosity of the party givers featured on these pages.

It is always a pleasure and an honor to work with exceptionally gifted people, especially when they are as enthusiastic and committed as photographer, Jerry Rabinowitz and stylist, Katherine Lande. Jerry devoted marathon hours to this project and I am so thankful for his talent, professionalism, and patience. Katherine added an element of beauty to these pages that so accurately captures each hosts personal style. I am so very grateful for their willingness to volunteer time and talent to this project.

The support of my beautiful family, greatest cheerleaders, and best tasters, made this project joyfully come to life. I am so thankful for their encouragement and participation in all I do. Gigi, Kayla, and Elisa, my partners in the kitchen, made cooking, tasting, and testing a celebration.

The Amory family has tasted and tested all of our recipes and I am in awe of their willingness to open both hearth and heart to this project. Their generosity and spirit of volunteerism knows no bounds.

To our gracious hosts who generously shared their beautiful homes, yachts, creative ideas, and their gracious hospitality in the spirit of giving: Thank you for your willingness to share food and wine, your treasured recipes, and to appear on these pages!

When Alain Ducasse agreed to write the foreword for this book it was the proverbial icing on the cake, a great thrill and honor, and I am so thankful for his thoughtful contribution.

Deep appreciation to my agent, Carla Glasser, and my extraordinary editors, Christopher Steighner and Tricia Levi, and their team at Rizzoli, for their hard work, dedication, and guidance, and for believing in this project.

Having Doug Turshen and his talented colleague, David Huang, as graphic designers on this project was literally a dream come true.

Special gratitude to the many friends who have helped along the way: Shamin Abas, Doreen Alfaro, Heather Archut, Paola Bacchini-Rosenshein, Merrilyn Bardes, Wendy Bazilian, Theresa Bischoff, John Bossard, Cora Brown, Liz Brown, Annharriet Buck, Rob Caldwell, Nancy Carter, Bonnie Clearwater, Patrick Enage, Shannon Felder, Donna Fields, Sandra Geraci Kaszak, Bon Hall, Sara B. Lerner, Elvia Lejarza, David Leverrier and Chez Jean-Pierre, Marta Malouf, Nicola Marcus, Brigitte Merey, Steve Myers, Stephen Myers, Jr., Tom Orlando, Mark Passler, Dennis Rivera, Carl Roston, Sean Rush, Marie Samuels, Florence Seiler, Robert Swinson, Amy Treitel, Mike Viars, Jayne Villamizar, Lucien Capehart photography, Tim Edwards Services, and *Palm Beach Illustrated* magazine.

ABOUT THE CONTRIBUTORS

VICTORIA AMORY
writes about food, style, and entertaining. Since 2002, she has published two award-winning cookbooks and produced editorials in numerous magazines and newspapers. Victoria was born in Spain, attended school in England, and lives between Florida and Connecticut with her husband and their three boys.

AIME DUNSTAN
is the founder and creative director of It! Weddings & Events. She has helmed countless soirees in Palm Beach and the Hamptons. A journalist by training, her work has been featured in *Hamptons Cottages & Gardens*, *Southern Accents*, *Coastal Living*, *Florida Travel + Life*, and *Quest* magazines. She lives in a historic West Palm Beach bungalow with her husband and son.

ANNIE FALK
conceives and co hosts fundraising events alongside the world's most recognized names in entertainment, fashion, and society. The private foundation she began with her husband is dedicated to improving the lives of children, protecting and preserving our natural environment, and responding to environmental emergencies that adversely affect families. A philanthropist, writer, and art collector, she lives in New York and South Florida with her family.

KATHERINE LANDE
is the fashion editor for *Palm Beach Illustrated* magazine. She is responsible for the conception, coordination, and creation of the covers, fashion spreads, and style-focused editorials. She founded KL Style, Inc., a fashion consulting and styling business serving private clients, companies, and events. Katherine resides in South Florida.

DAPHNE NIKOLOPOULOS
is the editor-in-chief of *Palm Beach Illustrated* magazine and the editorial director of Palm Beach Media Group. She is the author of *The Tenth Saint*, an archaeological thriller, and *The Storm Gourmet*, a hurricane-preparedness cookbook. Daphne has worked as a journalist in the U.S., U.K., and Greece. Born in Athens, Greece, she now resides in South Florida with her family.

JERRY RABINOWITZ
is an award-winning commercial and editorial photographer with 30 years of experience. He has taught and lectured for Fujifilm, Boston University, and Palm Beach Photographic Workshops. Jerry was president of A.S.M.P New Mexico and profiled in *Rangefinder* magazine. Specializing in architectural themes, lifestyle, and fine art photography, his assignments take him around the world, and his work regularly appears in national and regional publications, books, brochures, advertising campaigns, and annual reports. He lives in Delray Beach, FL.

CONVERSION CHART

All conversions are approximate.

LIQUID CONVERSIONS

U.S.	METRIC
1 tsp	5 ml
1 tbs	15 ml
2 tbs	30 ml
3 tbs	45 ml
1/4 cup	60 ml
1/3 cup	75 ml
1/3 cup + 1 tbs	90 ml
1/3 cup + 2 tbs	100 ml
1/2 cup	120 ml
2/3 cup	150 ml
3/4 cup	180 ml
3/4 cup + 2 tbs	200 ml
1 cup	240 ml
1 cup + 2tbs	275 ml
1 1/4 cups	300 ml
1 1/3 cups	325 ml
1 1/2 cups	350 ml
1 2/3 cups	375 ml
1 3/4 cups	400 ml
1 3/4 cups + 2 tbs	450 ml
2 cups (*1 pint*)	475 ml
1/2 cups	600 ml
3 cups	720 ml
4 cups (*1 quart*)	945 ml
	(*1,000 ml is 1 liter*)

WEIGHT CONVERSIONS

U.S./U.K.	METRIC
1/2 oz	14 g
1 oz	28 g
1 1/2 oz	43 g
2 oz	57 g
2 1/2 oz	71 g
3 oz	85 g
3 1/2 oz	100 g
4 oz	113 g
5 oz	142 g
6 oz	170 g
7 oz	200 g
8 oz	227 g
9 oz	255 g
10 oz	284 g
11 oz	312 g
12 oz	340 g
13 oz	368 g
14 oz	400 g
15 oz	425 g
1 lb	454 g

OVEN TEMPERATURES

°F	GAS MARK	°C
250	1/2	120
275	1	140
300	2	150
325	3	165
350	4	180
375	5	190
400	6	200
425	7	220
450	8	230
475	9	240
500	10	260
550	Broil	290

First published in the United States of America in 2012 by Rizzoli International Publications, Inc.
300 Park Avenue South
New York, NY 10010
www.rizzoliusa.com

© 2012 Annie Falk

2012 2013 2014 2015 / 10 9 8 7 6 5 4 3 2 1

Distributed in the U.S. trade by
Random House, New York
Printed in China

ISBN-13: 978-0-8478-3795-3

Library of Congress Catalog Control Number: 2012937148

Book design by Doug Turshen with David Huang

Portraits on pages 206, 207, 223: Lucien Capehart Photography

Portrait on page 174: Firooz Zahedi Photography

Portrait on page 209: Pamela Jones Photography